This book is to be returned on or before
the last date stamped below.

YOU CAN HELP!

Also by Richard Nelson-Jones and published by Cassell:

Effective Thinking Skills:
Preventing and Managing Personal Problems

Human Relationship Skills (2nd edition)

Lifeskills: A Handbook

Practical Counselling and Helping Skills:
How to Use the Lifeskills Helping Model (3rd edition)

The Theory and Practice of Counselling Psychology

Training Manual for Counselling and Helping Skills

YOU CAN HELP!

INTRODUCING LIFESKILLS HELPING

Dr Richard Nelson-Jones

CASSELL

Cassell
Villiers House, 41/47 Strand, London WC2N 5JE

387 Park Avenue South, New York, NY 10016-8810

First published 1993

British Library Cataloguing-in-Publication Data
A catalogue record for this book is available from the
British Library.

ISBN 0-304-32831-6

Typeset by Litho Link Ltd., Welshpool, Powys, Wales.
Printed and bound in Great Britain by Biddles Ltd,
Guildford and King's Lynn

Contents

	Preface	vii
1	Let's talk lifeskills	1
2	The lifeskills helping model	6
3	What you bring to helping	22
4	How to develop supportive helping relationships	33
5	How to identify and clarify problems	46
6	How to assess feelings	60
7	How to assess thinking skills	69
8	How to assess action skills	82
9	How to redefine problems in skills terms	89
10	How to state working goals	97
11	How to plan interventions	108
12	How to use training skills	116
13	How to focus on thinking skills	129
14	How to develop action skills	147
15	How to focus on feelings	162
16	How to consolidate self-helping skills	178
17	How to end helping	185
18	You can help!	191
	Selected bibliography	197
	Index	201

Preface

Welcome to *You Can Help!* In this book I aim to provide a brief, user-friendly introduction to lifeskills helping (LSH). Lifeskills helping offers a language, model and skills for becoming a more effective helper. Following are four key concepts of the lifeskills helping approach.

1. Most problems brought to helpers are educational in nature.
2. Though external factors contribute, clients sustain problems by possessing underlying thinking skills and action skills weaknesses.
3. Helpers are most effective when they flexibly use both good supportive relationship skills and good training skills.
4. The ultimate goal of lifeskills helping is self-helping, whereby clients maintain and develop thinking skills and action skills strengths, not just to cope with present problems, but to prevent and handle future similar problems.

Though it is an oversimplification, perhaps helpers may be divided into two broad categories: professional and non-professional. *You Can Help!* caters for non-professional helpers, such as students taking part-time counselling courses, or helping skills modules as part of other professional courses (for instance, nursing, teacher training or personnel management), or counselling modules as part of university or college of further education psychology and behavioural science courses; and those training for work in voluntary counselling agencies, for instance, marital work, pastoral care, AIDS/HIV counselling or bereavement counselling. In addition, *You Can Help!* may be of interest to lay readers wanting to help either others or themselves. The lifeskills helping approach is much more thoroughly presented in *Practical Counselling and Helping Skills: How to Use the Lifeskills Helping Model* (third edition), also published by Cassell. *Practical Counselling and Helping Skills* caters mainly for those using helping skills as a major part of their professional work: for instance, counselling psychologists, social workers and psychiatric nurses. A separate *Training Manual for Counselling and Helping Skills* is available to supplement both main and introductory texts and encourage learning by doing.

ORGANIZATION

Chapters 1 to 3 are introductory. Chapter 1 defines terms. In Chapter 2 I describe the lifeskills helping model. Chapter 3 looks at what students and helpers bring to their helping work. Chapters 4 to 17 systematically present the five stages of the model. Chapters 4 and 5 focus on the component skills of stage 1, which are to develop the relationship between helper and client and to identify and clarify problems. Chapters 6 to 9 present skills for stage 2: assessing and redefining problems in skills terms. Chapters 10 and 11 describe skills for stage 3: stating working goals and planning interventions. The next four chapters present the stage 4 skills of how to intervene to develop the client's self-helping skills. Chapters 16 and 17 present skills for stage 5: how to end helping and consolidate self-helping skills. The final chapter examines how you can assess and develop your lifeskills helping skills.

ACKNOWLEDGEMENTS

You will discover that lifeskills helping has its own language and ideas. Nevertheless, my approach owes much to others' work. I am very grateful to all those writers whose names are in the bibliography. Many thanks also to Naomi Roth, my Cassell editor, and to Windy Dryden for encouraging me when the idea of an introductory lifeskills helping text was barely a glint in my eye. In addition I warmly thank Sandra Margolies, of Cassell house editorial.

I hope you find that *You Can Help!* gives you more confidence and skills for helping others. I wish you well in your helping endeavours.

Richard Nelson-Jones

To the current generation of young helpers

ONE
Let's talk lifeskills

'Tis skill, not strength, that governs a ship.
Thomas Fuller

Lifeskills helping (LSH) is a people-centred approach for assisting clients and others to develop self-helping skills. The approach spurns psychological jargon in favour of a simple, direct, educational framework. Geared to the needs of the vast majority of ordinary people, lifeskills helping assumes that all people have acquired and sustain lifeskills strengths and weaknesses. Lifeskills helpers collaborate with clients to detect the lifeskills weaknesses that sustain problems and then, within supportive relationships, train them in relevant self-helping skills.

Below are some clients who bring problems to helpers:

Sandra, aged 8, is a primary-school student who is very retiring and finds it difficult to make friends.

Dean, aged 17, is a secondary-school student who is damaging his prospects of getting into his preferred university course by not performing up to his ability in some subjects.

A year ago Sally, aged 22, was grabbed in broad daylight by a man near a railway station. When she resisted him the man ran off. Now Sally reports being unreasonably aggressive towards males. Also, she has difficulty sleeping alone in the dark.

Pam and Scott, both in their mid-30s, have been married for over 12 years. They used to enjoy each other's company, but now say they communicate little about anything that matters.

Marcia, aged 41, has brought up three children, the oldest of whom is now 16. She wants to get back into the work force, but is terrified at the prospect.

Jon, aged 57, a foreman at a car factory, is recovering from a serious heart attack. He was overweight, smoked and drank heavily, and took little exercise. Jon is at risk of reverting to his former habits.

Betty, aged 64, a single career woman, retired six months ago after being head of the radiography department at a local hospital. She finds herself thoroughly bored with the lack of structure and social contacts in her life.

Tom, aged 78, is a widower whose wife died two years ago. Much of the time he feels depressed and apathetic. He used to be an enthusiastic gardener, but now does not even bother with that.

All the above clients are at different stages in life and have different problems. However, they all have one thing in common: namely, the need to develop lifeskills to deal with the challenges they face.

Lifeskills helping is about you and not just your clients. Helpers need lifeskills. We are all made of the same human clay. Sometimes you need to develop lifeskills in areas in which you function poorly: for example, public speaking. On other occasions, you can develop lifeskills in areas in which you function well, but wish to function better: for example, asserting yourself or managing anger. In addition, you need to develop your helping skills. However, some helping skills are similar to lifeskills you require at home, for instance listening skills. Here, developing lifeskills and developing helping skills overlap. Ideally, as helpers you are proficient in any lifeskills you impart to clients.

DEFINING LIFESKILLS

Lifeskills may be defined in three main ways: by area, by level of expertise, and by the choices entailed in carrying out the skill.

- *By area.* Lifeskills areas comprise the various self-helping skills through which people live effectively, for instance, specific job interview skills, stress management skills or relating skills. Virtually any skill, for instance, cooking, may be viewed as a lifeskill. However, lifeskills helping focuses in particular on skills containing a large psychological or 'mind' component in them.
- *By level.* People may exhibit different levels or degrees of skills or expertise in a lifeskills area. Usually, within a lifeskills area a person's level of competence is more complex than either good or bad: he or she possesses both strengths and weaknesses. For instance, within the overall skill of rewarding listening, you may be good at receiving messages accurately, but poor at responding in ways that show you have understood. The concept of level does not imply moral judgement: people may work to alter the balance of strengths and weaknesses in a skills area more than in the direction of strengths.
- *By choice.* Lifeskills can be viewed as choice processes. The essential element of any skilled performance, be it either managing anger or playing tennis, is the ability to make and implement a correct sequence of choices in a skills area. Good choices in skills areas are skills strengths and poor choices are skills weaknesses. Put simply, the criterion for skills strengths and skills weaknesses is whether they help or hinder people to assume personal responsibility for their happiness and fulfilment. Lifeskills helping aims to empower people by assisting them in making self-helping choices so that they become their own best helpers.

People require a repertoire of lifeskills. Such lifeskills may vary according to the developmental tasks they face throughout their life-spans: for instance, going to school for the first time, getting married, parenting, dealing with aged parents and facing their own deaths. In addition, people require lifeskills to deal with their specific problems of living, such as specific relationship difficulties, handling unemployment and dealing with physical disabilities. However, lifeskills helping can also assist people in developing and liberating their potentials. The approach has 'growth' as well as 'remedial' goals. Paradoxically, frequently real growth takes place when people face up to major problems and challenges.

Following is a brief positive definition of lifeskills:

Lifeskills are sequences of self-helping choices in specific psychological skills areas.

SKILLS LANGUAGE

Let's talk lifeskills. Skills language means consistently using the concept of skills to describe and analyse your own and client behaviours. Skills language is central to lifeskills helping. The theoretical framework for the approach is expressed in skills language. Helpers consistently think in and use skills language during helping. They encourage clients to think about problems in skills language not only during, but also after helping.

My guess is that currently you rarely, if ever, think of your own personal behaviour in skills language. Here is a brief illustration in an account from Henry, who puts into skills language what he did after waking up this morning.

When I woke up, I used my turning-off-the-alarm-clock skills. I then faced both my skills strengths and weaknesses in getting out of bed. Finally. I allowed my skills strengths to prevail, got out of bed and used my walking skills to go to the bathroom. When in the bathroom, I used my going-to-the-toilet, shaving and washing skills, before using my walking skills to go back to my bedroom, where I used my getting-dressed skills.

Welcome to the world of lifeskills.

ACTIVITY

1. Either on your own or with a partner:
   (a) spend two or three minutes describing in skills language what you did since waking up this morning; and afterwards
   (b) assess whether and how this activity has taught you something about how you currently think.

TWO

The lifeskills helping model

Problems are only opportunities in work clothes.
Henry J. Kaiser

A distinction exists between assisting clients in managing problems and helping them to alter the underlying problematic skills that sustain problems. Problem management models, such as those of Carkhuff and Egan, are useful, since frequently clients require help to manage immediate problems. However, a big drawback of such models is that they inadequately address the *repetition phenomenon* – the repetitive nature of many clients' problems. In the past clients may have repeated underlying self-defeating behaviours, or lifeskills weaknesses, and they are at risk of continuing to do so in future. An example of such vertical repetition across time is that of people who keep losing jobs because of poor relating-to-employers skills. Clients may also repeat self-defeating behaviours, or lifeskills weaknesses, horizontally across a range of current situations. For example, the same people may be non-assertive at home, at work, in leisure activities and so on. Clients require assistance in developing lifeskills strengths that last into the future and not just for managing specific current problems. In reality, practical considerations may limit how much attention helpers can pay to underlying lifeskills weaknesses.

DASIE: THE FIVE-STAGE MODEL

Hello DASIE! DASIE (Figure 2.1) is a systematic five-stage model for helping clients both to manage problems and to alter problematic lifeskills. The model provides a framework or set of guidelines for helper choices. The use of the acronym is deliberate, to assist beginning helping trainees in remembering the five stages when faced with the anxiety of working with clients for the first time. DASIE's five stages are:

D Develop the relationship, identify and clarify problems.
A Assess problem(s) and redefine in skills terms.
S State working goals and plan interventions.
I Intervene to develop self-helping skills.
E End and consolidate self-helping skills.

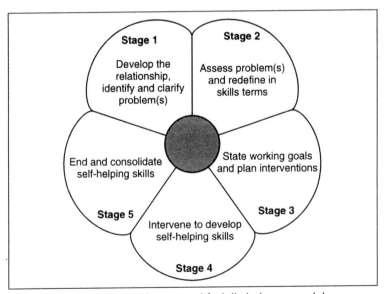

Figure 2.1   *DASIE: the five-stage lifeskills helping model*

STAGE 1   DEVELOP THE RELATIONSHIP, IDENTIFY AND CLARIFY PROBLEM(S)

Stage 1 starts with pre-helping contact with clients and either ends at some time in the initial interview or may take longer. It has two main overlapping functions: developing supportive helping relationships and working with clients to identify and obtain fuller descriptions of problems. Supportive helping relationships go beyond offering empathy, non-possessive warmth and genuineness to fostering client self-support more actively. The nature of the supportive relationship differs according to the stage of the model. In stage 1, helpers use relationship skills to provide emotional support as clients tell and elaborate their stories. In subsequent stages, helpers use relationship skills to support training interventions. At all stages, helpers combine and flexibly exhibit tough minds and tender hearts. Though lifeskills helping is basically a tough-minded approach, tenderness, gentleness, sensitivity and compassion for human frailty are highly valued so long as they are used in clients' best interests.

Many of the helper skills used in stage 1 are the same as those used in other approaches, for example, reflective responding, summarizing and confronting. Helpers collaborate with clients to explore, clarify and understand problems. Together they act as detectives to discover what clients' real problems and agendas are. Then they break these down into their component parts. An analogy for the role of questioning in initial sessions is that of plants and their root systems. For example, a client comes to helping saying 'I am depressed. Help me.' This statement about depression represents the above-ground part of the plant. However, by listening, observing and effective questioning, the helper starts identifying roots of the client's problem in five different areas: relates poorly to spouse, has a difficult parent, is short of friends, has few pleasant activities and gets little satisfaction from work. Now both helper and client have information about the overall problem's sub-structure so that they can develop hypotheses about how the client contributes to sustaining each problem area.

Helpers can use skills language when structuring initial sessions. One possibility is to start the session by giving clients an open-ended permission to tell their stories. After they respond, the following statement might structure the remainder of the session:

You've given me some idea of why you've come. Now I'd like to ask some more questions to help us to clarify your problem(s) [specify]. Then, depending on what we find, I shall suggest some skills to help you cope better. Once we agree on what skills might help you, then we can look at ways to develop them. Does this way of proceeding sound all right?

When structuring, helpers can briefly state reasons for adopting a lifeskills approach. Following are examples:

It can be useful to think of problems in terms of the skills you need to cope better. This way you get some 'handles' or leverage to work for change.

The approach I take assumes that most behaviour is learned. To work effectively on problems, people need to look at how they think and act. Unhelpful skills of thinking and acting can be unlearned and helpful skills learned.

Lifeskills helping distinguishes between inner-game skills, or thinking skills, and outer-game skills, or action skills. Thinking skills include: owning responsibility for choosing, coping self-talk, possessing realistic personal rules, perceiving accurately, attributing cause accurately, predicting realistically, goal setting and decision making. Such skills owe much to the work of Beck, Ellis and Meichenbaum. Action skills vary by area of application, such as parenting, test taking or going for a job interview. There are five main ways of sending action skills messages, namely verbal, voice, body and touch messages, and how you act when not in face-to-face contact.

A word about helper thinking skills in stage one: beginning trainees may especially need to focus on their inner games. For example, unrealistic rules about approval and achievement contribute to anxious interviewing. Helpers can use self-talk both to calm themselves down and to coach themselves. Helpers need awareness of personal barriers to perceiving clients accurately. Also, they need to recognize dividing lines between their own and clients' responsibilities.

As early as stage 1, helpers need to explore ways of enhancing their efficiency as psychological educators. A whiteboard is an essential tool for lifeskills helpers. For example, many clients understand problems better if their component parts are visually presented. Furthermore, clients can keep records of what helpers write. In addition, clients can be requested to listen at home to audio cassettes of their helping sessions. Learning can be further enhanced by other homework assignments, for instance, completing self-monitoring logs.

An illustrative summary of the same case ends each brief description of the DASIE model's stages:

> Rob and Betty are the parents of three girls, aged 15, 13 and 11, The precipitating crisis was that Rob struck his oldest daughter, Ruth, when she came home late from a date with her boyfriend. Rob comes to helping afraid his family may break up because of his temper outbursts. Betty supports Rob's coming for help, but does not wish to come too. The helper encourages Rob to describe how he and Ruth feel, think and act towards each other. Rob also shares his perceptions of how he and the other family members relate. Rob discloses a history of temper outbursts both at home and at work. The helper is alert for clues of thinking and action skills weaknesses. For instance, when Rob says that people stir him, he gives the impression that he has no choice over how he behaves. After a series of exploratory probes, interspersed with empathic reflections, the helper summarizes the content of the interview so far and checks Rob's reactions. Both the helper and Rob now have a broader understanding of the component parts of Rob's managing-anger problem.

STAGE 2   ASSESS PROBLEM(S) AND REDEFINE IN SKILLS TERMS

The object of this stage is to build a bridge between *describing* and *actively working on* problems and their underlying skills weaknesses. In stage 1, problems have been described, amplified and clarified, largely in everyday language. The description of clients' problems represents an expansion of their internal viewpoints rather than providing them with different insights. In stage 2, helpers build upon information collected in stage 1 to explore hypotheses about how clients think and act in ways that sustain difficulties. Helpers add to and go beyond clients' present perceptions to look for 'handles' on how to work for change. They collaborate to break down clients' problems into their component skills weaknesses. Whereas stage 1 might end with descriptive summaries of problems in everyday terms, stage 2 ends with a redefinition of at least either the main or the most pressing problem in skills terms.

The nature of the supportive relationship changes in stage 2. In stage 1, helpers support clients in telling their stories in their own terms. In stage 2, helpers support clients in making sense of their stories. A critical ingredient of stage 2 is for helpers to maintain a skills focus. This does not mean that helpers immediately translate everything clients say into skills language. However, the question at the back of helpers' minds in stage 2 is always 'What skills weaknesses sustain clients' problems?' Especially for beginning helpers, another question is 'If I identify skills weaknesses, do I possess the interventions to deal with them?' Many neophyte helpers possess very restructed repertoires of practical interventions, thus limiting their capacity both to formulate working definitions and to follow through on them. Most clients do not think of their problems in skills language, so helpers require sensitivity in when and how they convey that clients may have specific thinking and action skills weaknesses.

The emphasis in helpers' questions in stage 2 differs from that in stage 1. In stage 1, helpers ask questions to clarify clients' existing frames of reference. In stage 2, helpers are likely to question as much from their own as from their clients' frames of reference. Much questioning is based on information wittingly or unwittingly provided by clients – clues, hunches, how things are said, what is left unsaid, and overt and subtle indications of underlying thought patterns. While the major focus is on pinpointing skills weaknesses, attention is also paid to identifying skills strengths and resources. Strength reviews both identify skills for coping with problems and also prevent assessments from becoming too negative.

Helpers need to develop good skills at redefining problems in skills terms and communicating these working definitions to clients. A good redefinition succinctly suggests clients' main skills weaknesses that sustain problems. Helpers need to distinguish important from less important material. Redefinitions that are too comprehensive confuse. If they have not already done so, helpers can suggest the value of breaking problems down into the component skills that sustain them. Furthermore, they may introduce clients to the distinction between thinking skills and action skills, possibly using the analogy of the inner and outer games.

Often it helps to write redefinitions in skills terms on whiteboards. Visual communication makes it easier for clients to retain what you say and, if necessary, suggest alterations. Helpers may use a simple T diagram to present thinking- and action-skills weaknesses for sustaining each problem (see Figure 2.2). Redefinitions of problems in skills terms, otherwise known as T redefinitions or as 'Teeing up problems', need to be negotiated with clients. Helpers require good questioning and facilitation skills when checking redefinitions with clients. If helpers, in stages 1 and 2, have competently gathered information, skills redefinitions should flow reasonably logically from this material. Clients who share their helpers' conceptualizations of problems are more likely to commit themselves to developing needed

Problem

Thinking-skills weaknesses	Action-skills weaknesses

Figure 2.2 *A simple T diagram for presenting redefinitions of problems in skills terms*

self-helping skills than clients resisting helpers' conceptualizations. Redefinitions of problems in skills terms are essentially hypotheses, based on careful analysis of available information, about clients' thinking- and action-skills weaknesses. As hypotheses they are open to modification in the light of further or better information. Redefining problems in skills terms can be difficult. Mistakes in redefinition not only lead to time and effort being wasted, but may contribute to clients being even less able to manage problems.

After checking his descriptive summary, Rob's helper said he would now like to explore some specific areas of how Rob thought and acted to see if they could discover some skills he might use to improve his situation. The helper observed that some things Rob said indicated he experienced himself as having little choice over how he behaved. Rob agreed he had little control over his temper and wondered if it were his nature. The helper explored what Rob said to himself when faced with provocations, for example, his daughter Ruth coming home later than agreed. Rob's self-talk appeared to fire him up rather than calm him down. The helper also examined the realism of Rob's rules concerning family behaviour. Because the action skills of how Rob communicated with his family had already been covered in stage 1, the helper did not repeat this.

Using the whiteboard, the helper suggested the following T redefinition of Rob's problem in managing anger with his daughter. The *thinking-skills* weaknesses hypotheses were: (1) inadequately acknowledging that he was always a chooser and responsible for this thoughts, feelings and actions; (2) using anger-engendering self-talk when faced with provocations; and (3) possibly possessing rigid and unrealistic personal rules concerning standards of behaviour in the family. The *action-skills* weaknesses hypotheses were: (1) poor listening skills, especially when angry; (2) poor assertion skills, for instance, in how he stated his wishes about his daughter's behaviour; and (3) poor skills at working through conflicts with others. The helper checked each part of this working definition with

Rob to see whether he understood it and also whether he agreed with it. Rob expressed relief when the redefinition in skills terms was explained to him since, for the first time, he thought he could do something about his temper.

STAGE 3   STATE WORKING GOALS AND PLAN INTERVENTIONS

Stage 3 builds on your redefinitions in skills terms to focus on the question, 'What is the best way to manage problems and develop the requisite skills?' Stage 3 consists of two phases: stating working goals and planning interventions.

Stating working goals

Goals can be stated at different levels of specificity. First, goals can be stated in overall terms, such as, 'I want to feel less depressed', 'I want to improve my marriage', or 'I want to come to terms with my disability and get back into life.' Such overall goals statements give clients visions about what they want from helping. However, overall statements refer more to ends than to means. Second, goals can be stated in terms of the broad skills required to attain ends. This level of specificity is required for stage 3. Assuming you succeed in redefining problems in skills terms, stating goals becomes a relatively simple matter. Working goals are the flip-side of your redefinitions: positive statements of skills strengths to replace existing skills weaknesses. For instance, if part of the skills redefinition of Annie's problem is that she has poor job-seeking skills, developing job-seeking skills becomes her working goal.

Third, goals can be stated still more specifically. For example, Annie's job-seeking skills could be broken down into such subskills as how to telephone prospective employers, develop a resumé, conduct newspaper searches, handle interviews, deal with rejections and so on. Helpers have to decide the level of detail with which to share goals in early sessions. Each case requires being treated on its merits. Clients can only cope with so much information at any one time. A risk of getting into too much detail in an initial session is that clients retain little if anything. Helpers need to state working goals clearly and succinctly. If they are using whiteboards, helpers can alter existing skills redefinitions so that these become working goals. Helpers also need to ensure that clients understand and agree with working goals.

Planning interventions

Statements of working goals provide bridges to choosing interventions. Helpers as practitioner-researchers hypothesize not only about goals, but also about ways to attain them. An important distinction exists between interventions and plans. Interventions are intentional behaviours, on the part of either helpers or clients, designed to help clients attain problem-management and problematic-skills goals. Plans are statements of how to combine and sequence interventions to attain working goals.

Clients come to helping with a wide variety of problems, expectations, motivations, priorities, time constraints and lifeskills strengths and weaknesses. Helpers tailor intervention plans to individual clients. In very focused helping – say, anxiety about an imminent test – helpers are likely to plan to manage the immediate problem, with less emphasis on altering underlying problematic skills. With more time to alter problematic skills, helpers may choose between structured plans and open plans. Structured plans are step-by-step training and learning outlines of interventions for attaining specific goals. Sometimes structured plans involve using existing material, for instance, developing relaxation skills using a programme based on Bernstein and Borkovec's *Progressive Relaxation Training: A Manual for the Helping Professions*. Helpers and clients can also design partially structured plans to attain working goals. For instance, in the case of a recently fired executive, certain sessions might be set aside for testing to assess interests and aptitudes and for attending a brief course to develop specific action skills, such as resumé writing and interview skills. Agendas for the remaining sessions are negotiated at the start of each session.

Open plans without predetermined structure allow helpers and clients to choose which interventions to use to attain which working goals and when. Open plans have the great advantage of flexibility. Clients may be more motivated to work on skills and material relevant at any given time than to run through predetermined programmes independent of current considerations. Furthermore, owing to the frequently repetitive nature of clients' skills weaknesses, work done in one session may be highly relevant to work done on the same or different problems in other sessions.

> The helper clarified that Rob's overall goal was to improve his relationship with Ruth and hence improve his family life. Using the whiteboard, he turned the redefinition of Rob's anger problem into a T statement of working goals. Rob's *thinking-skills* goals were: (1) to acknowledge that he was a chooser responsible for his thoughts, feelings and actions; (2) to use coping self-talk when faced with provocations; and (3) to develop realistic personal rules concerning standards for family behaviour. Rob's *action-skills* goals included developing: (1) good listening skills; (2) assertion skills, with specific reference to how he stated his wishes about his daughter's behaviour; and (3) conflict-negotiation skills.
>
> The helper realized that Rob's objective was to develop some skills as quickly as possible rather than to have a long-term helping relationship. He suggested the best plan was to use the material Rob brought into each session to develop targeted thinking and action skills. The helper required homework, including listening to audio cassettes of their sessions. He asked Rob to monitor how he communicated to Ruth and other family members and report back in the next session. Also, he provided Rob with a log to fill in about how he thought, felt and acted before, during and after specific anger provocations.

STAGE 4 INTERVENE TO DEVELOP SELF-HELPING SKILLS

The interventions stage has two objectives: first, to help clients manage their presenting problems better, and second, to assist clients in working on problematic skills and in developing skills strengths. Helpers are psychological educators. To intervene effectively they require good helping relationship skills and good training skills. It is insufficient to know *what* interventions to offer without also being skilled at *how* to offer them. Skilled helpers strike an appropriate balance between relationship and task orientations; less skilled helpers err in either direction.

Table 2.1 depicts modes of psychological education or training and modes of learning in lifeskills helping. Helpers work much of the time with the three training modes of 'tell', 'show' and 'do'. They require special training skills for each. 'Tell' entails giving clients clear instructions concerning the skills they wish to develop. 'Show' means providing demonstrations of how to implement skills. 'Do' means arranging for clients to perform structured activities and homework tasks.

Individual sessions in the intervention stage may be viewed in four often overlapping phases: preparatory, initial, working and ending. The preparatory phase entails helpers thinking in advance how best to assist clients. Helpers ensure that, if appropriate, they have available session plans, training materials such as handouts, and audiovisual aids such as whiteboards and audio-cassette recorders. The initial phase consists of meeting, greeting and seating, then giving permission to talk. Though it is a skill not restricted to the initial phase, early on helpers may wish to negotiate session agendas. For instance, helpers may go from checking whether the client has any current pressing agendas, to reviewing the past week's homework, to focusing on one or more problematic skills and/or problems in client's lives. As necessary, agendas may be altered during sessions.

Within a supportive relationship, the working phase focuses on specific thinking-skills and action-skills interventions designed to help clients manage problems and develop lifeskills. Thinking-skills interventions tend to entail three steps: increasing awareness of targeted thinking-skills weaknesses, challenging faulty thinking, and training in effective thinking. Action-skills interventions range from role-play rehearsals inside helping to conducting experiments in which clients try out changes in behaviour outside helping. Interventions focused on experiencing, expressing or managing feelings usually combine thinking- and action-skills interventions. The ending phase lasts from towards the end of one session to the beginning of the next. This phase focuses on summarizing the major session learnings, negotiating homework, strengthening commitment to between-session work, and rehearsing and practising skills outside helping. Consolidating learned skills as self-helping skills takes place at the end of and between each session. Frequently clients are asked to

Table 2.1 *Modes of psychological education or training and of learning*

Psychological education or training mode	Learning mode
Facilitate	Learning from self-exploring and from experiencing self more fully
Assess	Learning from self-evaluating and from self-monitoring
Tell	Learning from hearing
Show	Learning from observing
Do	Learning from doing structured activities and homework tasks
Consolidate	Learning from developing self-helping skills in all the above modes

fill out homework sheets. Providing written homework instructions serves the purposes of giving a message that homework is important, clarifying what is required, helping clients' memories, and providing something in writing that can be posted as a reminder.

Over a two-and-a-half month period, the helper saw Rob for a total of seven sessions, with the intervention stage lasting from the second to the sixth session. The helper's considerations in establishing session agendas included both where Rob wanted to focus and also how best to train Rob in targeted self-helping skills. When working on both thinking- and action-skills goals, the helper made extensive use of the whiteboard. Rob was trained in the *thinking-skills* goal that he was a chooser, partly by articulating this as a valuable skill, partly by encouraging him to become more aware of the consequences of his choices, partly by reframing his language – for example, 'Ruth made me so angry' was reformulated into 'I chose to get very angry with Ruth' – and partly by reflective responses that continuously and unobtrusively emphasized personal responsibility. Rob was trained in coping self-talk skills by the helper spending part of an early session directly instructing, demonstrating and coaching him. In subsequent sessions, the helper checked how well Rob used coping self-talk skills outside helping. The helper trained Rob in the skill of choosing realistic personal rules by assisting him to identify, dispute and reformulate inappropriate rules.

By means of instruction, demonstration, coached practice, and homework, the helper trained Rob in some simple listening *action skills* – for instance, not interrupting and checking how well he understood Ruth's position – as well as in skills of making assertive requests and negotiating conflicts. The helper encouraged Rob to 'learn on the job' by practising his skills at home. Rob's wife and daughters appreciated his genuine efforts to work on his temper. Even early on, his efforts were rewarded by less family tension.

STAGE 5   END AND CONSOLIDATE SELF-HELPING SKILLS

Most often, either helpers or clients bring up the topic of ending before the final session. This allows both parties to work through the various task and relationship issues connected with ending the contact. A useful option is to fade contact with some clients by seeing them progressively less often. Certain clients may appreciate the opportunity for booster sessions, perhaps one, two, three or even six months later. These provide both clients and helpers with the chance to review progress and consolidate self-helping skills. Scheduling follow-up telephone calls can perform some of these functions too.

Lifeskills helping seeks to avoid the 'train and hope' approach. For instance, prior to the ending stage, helpers structure realistic expectations when discussing working definitions and goals with clients. Also, helpers attempt to build client self-observation and assessment skills. Transfer and maintenance of skills is encouraged by such means as developing client's self-instructional abilities, working with real-life situations during helping, and using between-session time productively to listen to session cassettes and to rehease and practise skills. In addition, helpers can work with clients to anticipate difficulties and setbacks. Then together they can develop and rehearse coping strategies for preventing and managing lapses and relapses. Sometimes clients require help in identifying people to support their efforts to maintain skills. Helpers may also provide information about further skills-building opportunities.

During the sixth session, the helper and Rob decided to have one more session in four weeks' time on the helper's return from an overseas trip. Rob perceived he had lost some influence in the family by being more conciliatory when provoked. Using the whiteboard, the helper developed with Rob a balance sheet of positive and negative consequences of using his targeted skills. Rob thought the balance was heavily in favour of maintaining them. Rob started the seventh session by stating that his life was going much better. The helper assisted Rob in making clear connections between his improved family life, including his much better relationship with Ruth, and using his targeted skills. Rob observed that now he was much more likely to think first and then talk concerns over with family members. He thought there were still problems in his marriage, but did not wish to work on them at present. The helper left it open for Rob to return if he wanted. Three months later Rob sent the helper a Christmas card stating his family life continued to go well.

APPLYING THE MODEL

Helpers, in the best interests of clients, need to apply the DASIE helping model flexibly. Managing problems and altering problematic skills rarely proceed according to neatly ordered stages. Instead, stages tend to overlap, and helpers may revert to earlier stages as more information or new problems emerge.

DASIE is a model of central tendency. It assumes that much helping is relatively short-term, say three to ten sessions, and tends to be focused on one or two main problems and problematic skills areas. However, helping can also be very brief (say one or two sessions) or more extended (ten to twenty sessions or more). In both brief and extended helping, helpers need to adjust how person-oriented or task-oriented to be. In brief helping an early skills focus may be inappropriate, for example, with recently bereaved clients needing space to tell their stories and experience their grief. On the other hand, an immediate skills focus may be highly appropriate with clients anxious about upcoming job interviews. Since different reasons exist for extended helping, there are no simple answers for how best to go about it. Vulnerable clients may require more gentle and nurturing relationships than robust clients and take longer to attain insight into how they sustain problems. However, it is possible to over-generalize. From the initial session, some vulnerable clients may appreciate identifying and working on one or two specific skills weaknesses.

The DASIE helping model requires helpers to possess effective inner-game or thinking skills as well as effective outer-game or action skills. Helpers need to step outside everyday language to conceptualize problems in skills terms, and to possess both good supportive relationship skills and good training skills. In addition, lifeskills helpers require a range of specific interventions related to clients' problems and problematic skills. Building a reportoire of interventions takes time and effort – proficiency in lifeskills helping is a lifetime challenge.

ACTIVITY

1. Either on your own or with a partner:
   (a) assess the advantages and disadvantages of helpers working with systematic multi-stage models of the helping process; and
   (b) describe your initial thoughts and feelings about the lifeskills helping model.

THREE

What you bring to helping

Wherever we go, whatever we do,
self is the sole subject we study and learn.
Ralph Waldo Emerson

Helping differs from other occupations in that its main tool are people. When helpers and clients meet, each brings a wealth of personal characteristics and experiences. This chapter encourages you to become more aware of significant personal characteristics that you bring to training and helping.

YOUR MOTIVES

What motivates you to help? Often gaining insight into motivation is difficult, as motives can be complex, and you may deceive yourself. Many people entering helper training courses say, 'I want to help people' or 'People find me a good listener'. Your motives for being a helper may be helpful or harmful or, more likely, mixed. The criterion for a helpful motive is whether its consequences are in the best interests of clients. As with overall motivation, specific motives may be both helpful and harmful. Also, you may change over time – some helpers grow on the job, others do not.

Following are some helper motives that may work in clients' best interests. First, you may be altruistic or unselfishly concerned with others' welfare. Some of you may work for the betterment of others because of your religion, and altruism represents the concept

(Christian, though not only so) of *agape* or unselfish love. However, selfless instincts usually require self-discipline to sustain them. Second, you may hold humanistic values. Humanism entails belief in the possibility of reason overcoming anxiety, fear and destructive tendencies, and your humanism may commit you to the struggle to improve yourself and others. Third, your personality type may suit you for helping. Personality types result from differences in people's heredity and experiences, and American psychologist John Holland asserts that the social personality type is likely to be found in the helping professions. Characteristics of this type are being responsible, helpful, friendly, idealistic, feminine, insightful and kind. Helpers tend to be people who like working with people.

Fourth, you may have experienced significant emotional pain. Emotional pain can be for good or ill. If you have worked through your pain, you may be more compassionate towards others than if you had led a more tranquil life. In addition, you may have acquired some useful helping skills and insights from being in the client role. Early in my helping career, I learned much from being a client. Fifth, you may have a great interest in 'what makes people tick'. Good helpers constantly test and refine hypotheses about human behaviour, specific clients and the helping process. Sixth, you may have a commitment to competence. You may take pride in your work and not be prepared to settle for less than your best. Professional integrity is another term for commitment to competence.

Potentially harmful motives have the common thread that, in varying degrees, they lead to clients being treated as objects rather than as persons. For instance, helpers with unresolved personal agendas may seek to control clients rather than respect them as separate individuals. Insufficient self-acceptance can lead to insidious lack of acceptance of others. You may be a 'do-gooder' who needs dependent and appreciative clients, or you may seek intimacy from clients that you cannot attain elsewhere. Carl Rogers, the founder of person-centred counselling, admits that his interest in helping grew in part out of his early loneliness and that it provided a socially approved way of getting really close to others. Where Rogers used his loneliness as a springboard to personal growth, others may be less honest and less prepared to work on themselves. Some helpers restrict their awareness of clients through distortedly seeing them through the spectacles of a cause about which they feel strongly, be it psychoanalysis, religion or the rights of specific minority groups. They selectively perceive clients' problems to fit their pet frameworks. Some people enter helping as a ticket to an easy life. Motivated by expediency rather than genuine commitment, they resemble the client who, after remaining silent from the start of helping, interrupted the fourth session to ask his helper, 'Do you by any chance need a partner?'

What are your potentially helpful and harmful motives for being a helper? How can you shift your balance of motives more in the direction of helpful motives?

YOUR HELPING EXPERIENCES

Your past helping experiences fall into two main categories: being helped and helping others. Throughout your life many people have tried to help you – parents, siblings, teachers, friends and partners. In addition, you may have experienced professional helping. Probably, without always being aware, you have acquired some skills strengths and weaknesses from observing and being the recipient of others' helping behaviours. For example, because of your prior experience, you may think the way to help is to be quick to give advice. Even worse, you may put others down when giving advice, for example, 'Don't feel so sorry for yourself', or 'Don't be such a wimp'. Alternatively, having been sensitively listened to yourself, you may want to pass on this precious gift to others.

At many times in your life you have tried to help others. Which of your behaviours did you find rewarding? Also, which of your behaviours helped or harmed others, and how do you know? Once in training, many people become surprised at how difficult it is to offer good helping skills.

YOUR THINKING SKILLS

Skilled helpers possess good thinking skills. When you were growing up, you not only learned how to act, you also learned how to think. You bring your inner game or how you think to helping. You may find it difficult to think about how you think, perhaps because of never having realized the importance of this before, not knowing how to do it, or letting anxiety interfere.

Since thinking skills are covered in more detail elsewhere, I mention them only briefly here. The following are four areas in which you may possess weaknesses as well as strengths:

- *Using coping self-talk.* Please carry out the following instructions now: 'Close your eyes for thirty seconds and think of nothing'. Almost certainly, you found that you could not banish your voice from your head, for throughout your waking hours you continually talk to yourself. Most people engage in some negative self-talk that contributes to unwanted feelings and actions. For example, Sharon may tell herself before interviewing her first client, 'I'm inadequate', 'I have little to offer' and 'The client will think me incompetent'. Alternatively, and better, Sharon could engage in coping self-talk in which she calms herself down and coaches herself in the skills she needs.

- *Choosing realistic personal rules.* Each person has a rule book of personal rules for living, which are the standards and beliefs by which each of us lives. Sharon may possess one or more unrealistic personal rules that contribute to her negative self-talk. Such rules tend to be over-generalizations starting with words like 'should', 'ought' and 'must'. For instance, Sharon may believe, 'I *must* always have my clients' approval' or 'I *must* never make mistakes'. Such rules are self-defeating because they place her under too much pressure. Whether or not clients approve or she makes mistakes, all Sharon can do is the best she can.

- *Perceiving accurately.* You bring to helping your skills of perceiving yourself and your clients accurately. Central to this is the ability to distinguish fact from inference. For example, Sharon may possess adequate skills for her stage of helper training, yet unrealistically perceive that she possesses hardly any skills. Sharon inaccurately perceives both her present skills level and how long it takes to acquire fluent skills. Also, because she is nervous, Sharon risks inaccurately perceiving her client. In addition, like virtually all helpers, Sharon may bring many biases and filters to how she perceives clients.

- *Attributing responsibility accurately.* Rogers' person-centred counselling approach is based on the assumption that helpers should allow clients to take responsibility for their lives rather than be controlled and directed by helpers. If anything, beginning helpers assign to themselves too much rather than too little responsibility for the outcomes of helping. Ways in which helpers assume too much responsibility include listening too little, questioning too much and making premature suggestions.

YOUR FEELINGS

You bring to helping your capacity to experience your feelings. Feelings are physical sensations representing your underlying animal nature, so you are a continuous flow of biological experiencing. While you may be aware of many of your feelings, you may also deny and distort some of them. To the extent that you are out of touch with your feelings, you are alienated from the core of your personhood. Furthermore, how responsive you are to your own feelings can influence how responsive you are to clients' feelings. If you are distant from your own feelings, clients' feelings may not resonate accurately in you, thus making it difficult for you to understand them.

Your sense of worth is central to how you feel about yourself. Confidence and self-esteem are general traits and also vary across specific situations that people face. In varying degrees, all helpers possess some unresolved pain and unfinished business from their families of origin. How much you accept and respect yourself influences how much you accept and respect clients. You may send either affirming or damaging messages; effective helpers send more affirming messages then ineffective helpers. How do you think your sense of worth influences what messages you send to clients about their worth?

Both helper and client anxiety is always present in helping encounters. Anxiety may be defined as your fears about your capacity to cope adequately with the future. A close connection exists between your sense of worth and how anxious you are; insecurity both shows and produces anxiety. Beginning helpers bring their general level of anxiety to helping as well as their specific fears and anxieties about it. Anxiety can have positive and negative consequences. A certain level of anxiety tones helpers up and motivates them to give skilled performances, but excessive anxiety may lead to negative behaviours such as talking too much, responding inaccurately, asking too many questions, and being too controlling of how clients behave inside and outside helping.

Assuming the availability of skilled counsellors, probably most trainee helpers would profit from personal counselling to increase their sense of worth and decrease their anxieties and lifeskills weaknesses.

YOUR SEXUALITY

All helpers are sexual beings with differences in libido strength and in the extent to which they experience and express sexual feelings. Much of the variation in people's sexuality reflects learned inhibitions and prohibitions. Hopefully, your attitude towards your sexuality is healthy and loving. Sexual ignorance and poor thinking skills can interfere with helpers' effectiveness in their personal and professional lives. For instance, some helpers find it difficult to raise or talk about sexual matters with clients. Also, many helpers find it difficult to avoid dual relationships and sexual intimacy with them.

Are you straight, gay or in between? Erotic orientation is a complex area. Genetic and pre-natal influences interact with learning and socio-cultural factors. Most helpers are straight, but the many who are gay or bisexual are confronted with choices in their personal lives about how to handle homosexual feelings, whether to engage in homosexual sex and whether to 'come out' openly. All helpers have attitudes to clients' sexual orientation, whether it be the same as or different from their own. Furthermore, they possess varying degrees of knowledge about the psychology and behaviour of people of different sexual orientation. Especially if you plan to work in such areas as marital counselling, pregnancy counselling, sexual dysfunction counselling or counselling gay and bisexual people, you need to review the adequacy of your knowledge and attitudes about sexuality and sexual orientation.

YOUR SEX-ROLE IDENTITY AND EXPECTATIONS

Following are stipulated definitions relevant to your exploring your sex-role identity and expectations:

- *Sex*. Here sex refers to biological differences between males and females, for instance, differences in genitals, reproductive functions, bone structure and size.

- *Gender.* Gender refers to the social and cultural classification of attributes, attitudes and behaviours as 'feminine' or 'masculine'.
- *Gender awareness.* This relates to how aware you are of the processes and consequences of gender scripting on both females and males.
- *Sex-role identity.* Your sex-role identity is how you view yourself and behave on the dimensions of 'masculinity' and 'femininity'.
- *Sex-role expectations.* These are your thoughts and feelings about how you and others should think, feel and act on account of differences in biological sex.
- *Sexism.* Sexism relates to any feelings, thoughts and actions that assume the superiority of one sex over the other.

Sex roles based on gender learning influence how you perceive and behave. The consensus among social scientists seems to be that humans have weak instinctual remnants towards either a male or female sex-role identity and that biological predispositions may be easily overwhelmed by learning experiences. Your gender scripting started at the cradle with pink for girls and blue for boys. In Western society few people grow up without a considerable amount of gender brainwashing. Your current sex-role identity is the internalized sum of this brainwashing plus any modifications from countervailing experiences and from thinking for yourself.

The traditional feminine sex role may create problems for many women in such areas as expressing anger, autonomy, and obtaining and managing power and status. The traditional masculine sex role may create problems for many men through over-concern with success and power, competitiveness, emotional inexpressiveness, and restricting closeness between males. The concept of psychological androgyny grows in popularity because of sex-role shortcomings. The androgynous male or female is flexibly masculine or feminine as circumstances warrant. However, androgyny needs to take into account genetic differences in 'feminity' and 'masculinity'.

Helpers need to go beyond avoiding sexism to understanding the gender-scripting context of many clients' problems. Sex-role expectations may become intrusive in numerous ways. For instance, you may assess clients differently according to whether or not they fit into traditional sex roles, or you may bring to helping inflexible and sexist assumptions about appropriate behaviour in dating, mating and parenting. Your attitudes to sexual harassment, sexual abuse, rape and domestic violence may be sexist, or you may possess unexamined sexist assumptions about the place of males and females in the home or workforce and about jobs and careers appropriate for each sex. Both sexes may make sexist assumptions.

YOUR VALUES AND ETHICS

Your values are what you hold of worth, and represent the desirable means and ends of action. One way to think of values is in terms of a hierarchy ranked in terms of importance, another is to think of yourself as having a profile of values. Illustrative values include survival, friendship, family life, religion, materialism, aesthetics, social consciousness, career orientation, hedonism, nature and tradition. Helpers tend to place a high value on self-actualization or being committed to the personal growth and development of both themselves and their clients. You need to be aware of the significant values you bring to helping. Then you can choose how to handle them.

You also bring your value conflicts to helping – for instance, you may feel conflicted about charging fees for helping – or your values may conflict with clients' values – for instance, what are your attitudes towards pre-marital sex, extra-marital sex and homosexuality? For Catholic helpers, issues of contraception, abortion, divorce and intentional single parenting can create value conflicts. You bring to helping a style of handling value conflicts with others, for instance, avoiding conflicts, discussing them rationally, or aggressively pushing your values. Referral to helpers with more similar values is one option for handling severe value conflicts with clients. Another is to declare your values as your own and possibly use this as a springboard for helping clients to clarify their values.

Ethics and values are interrelated. Professional ethics issues abound in helper training as well as in later practice. Commitment to competence is a basic issue for helping students, but unfortunately, students have varying degrees of commitment to competence and of awareness of their shortcomings:

Each week, as part of her counselling skills practicum contract, Shirley is required to spend two hours outside class practising her skills. Despite the fact that her skills

need improvement, Shirley rarely bothers to practise. She
wants to pass the course with minimum effort.

Because Jack is on placement in a college counselling
service, his supervisor asks him to read up on different
interventions for examination anxiety. Jack does not do
this.

Ross has just seen a client who masturbates in the local
public library when reading erotic material. Ross tells
some of his friends about his client.

Allied to working on helping skills is the area of working on
potentially damaging aspects of yourself that you bring to helping. An
ethical commitment to helping entails not just working on your outer-
game or action skills, but having the courage to confront your inner-
game or thinking-skills weaknesses. Methods of confronting personal
weaknesses range from learning helping skills in self-referent ways
through self-helping and good supervision to personal counselling.
Awareness of areas of fallibility is the first step in preventing ethical
lapses.

YOUR CULTURE, RACE AND SOCIAL CLASS

Culture refers to a group's predominant values and patterns of
behaviour during a given period. Culture pervades every aspect of
living: language, food, religion, attitudes towards democracy, social
relations and work practices, to mention but some. Britain's ethnic
minority population is approximately 5 per cent of its total population,
with people of Pakistani, Bangladeshi and West Indian origin forming
large parts of this minority. Many in the ethnic minority population
were born outside Britain and feel the tension of adjusting to a
different culture. Their locally born and educated children may feel
caught between their parents' culture and the dominant culture.

You bring your degree of culture awareness to helping. Without
knowing it, you may possess cultural tunnel vision. You also bring your
cultural assumptions to helping, and a useful dictinction here is that
between culture-deficit and culture-sensitive assumptions. The
culture-deficit model assumes that the rules and values of the
dominant culture are normal and variations observed in minorities are

deficits. The culture-sensitive helping model avoids the assumption that dominant group practices are proper and superior; respect is shown for cultural differences, and positive features of cultural variation may be emphasized. You also bring your cross-cultural skills to helping. For instance, if you show interest and give people from different cultures permission to talk about the role of culture in their problems, you may be perceived as more empathic and culturally competent than if you are culture-neutral or culture-blind.

You bring your race and racial attitudes to helping. Racial differences are often highlighted by cultural differences. Approximately 95 per cent of the British population is white. Racism refers to the belief in the superiority of one race over another or others. In varying degrees, some helper trainees may possess racist attitudes, and some may be inadequately aware of the impact of race on ethnic minority clients' identity and life chances. Helpers possess different levels of racial mistrust and attraction, and different levels of racial empathy.

Income, educational attainment and occupational status are three of the main ways social class is measured in Britain. Other indicators are your accent, how you dress, where you went to school and where you live. You bring to helping your skills at understanding people from different social classes and of forming helping relationships with them. A common stereotype is the middle-class helper who lacks the language, life experience and skills to relate to lower-class clients. You need to develop social class-sensitive and race-sensitive skills along with culture-sensitive ones.

ACTIVITY

1. Either on your own or with a partner:
   (a) evaluate yourself on each of the following characteristics you bring to helping; and
   (b) assess how each characteristic may influence how you work as a helper:

   my motives;
   my helping experiences;
   my thinking skills;
   my feelings;

FOUR

How to develop supportive helping relationships

*The reason why we have two ears and only one mouth
is that we may listen the more and talk the less.*
Zeno of Citium

The next two chapters present skills for stage 1 of the lifeskills helping
model: develop the relationship, identify and clarify problem(s) (see
figure 4.1). This chapter emphasizes using rewarding listening skills

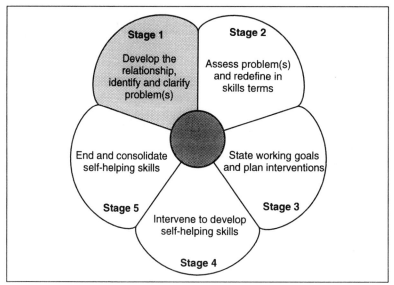

Figure 4.1   *Stage 1 Develop the relationship, identify and clarify
problem(s)*

to develop the helping relationship. Chapter 5 presents a range of skills for assisting clients in identifying and clarifying problems.

IMPORTANCE OF SUPPORTIVE HELPING RELATIONSHIPS

Supportive helper–client relationships assist clients to get the most out of helping in three main ways: by attending, by disclosing and by working. First, obvious as it may seem, you cannot help clients who are not there. If you fail to establish rapport with clients, you may not see them again. Second, if your rewarding listening skills are poor, clients may be less able to experience and explore their feelings. Also, they may reveal less to you. Without good listening skills you lower both your knowledge base and your influence.

Third, you need to support clients as they work to unlearn skills weaknesses and develop skills strengths. Lifeskills helpers are trainers and educators as well as facilitators. They have task orientations as well as person orientations. Helpers are more likely to develop clients' self-helping skills within the context of supportive helping relationships. Clients need support as they increasingly own responsibility for existing skills weaknesses, struggle during sessions to understand and practise new skills, and then risk using targeted skills in daily life. The remainder of this chapter focuses on the component skills of rewarding listening. Such skills assist clients in attending, disclosing and working. Ten skills of rewarding listening follow.

SKILL 1   KNOW THE DIFFERENCE BETWEEN ME AND YOU

Think of people you know who are good and poor listeners. Probably a key feature of all your poor listeners is that they fail to distinguish between their internal viewpoints and your internal viewpoint. If you respond to what speakers say in ways that show accurate understanding of their viewpoints, you respond 'as if' inside their internal viewpoints. You acknowledge the separateness between 'me' and 'you' by understanding 'where they are' rather than by imposing 'where you are' on them.

Below are two examples of helpers responding to the same client statement from external and internal viewpoints:

Client to employment counsellor

Client	I'm fed up with being unemployed.
Counsellor (external)	How hard have you looked for work?
Counsellor (internal)	You're exasperated with being out of work.

Client to school counsellor

Client	I'm pessimistic about passing my driving test.
Counsellor (external)	You've got no reason to doubt your driving ability.
Counsellor (internal)	You think the odds are you will fail your test.

Think of a three-link chain: client statement–helper response–client statement. If helpers respond from clients' internal viewpoints, they allow clients either to continue on the same path or to change direction. However, if helpers respond from their external viewpoints, they risk blocking clients by taking them in directions they would not have gone on their own. Helper responses move from being 'client-centred' to become more 'helper-centred'. Sometimes such external influence is desirable, but frequently it is not. In all instances, helpers need to make conscious choices whether or not to respond as if inside clients' internal viewpoints.

SKILL 2   POSSESS AN ATTITUDE OF RESPECT AND ACCEPTANCE

Helpers need to respect clients as separate and unique human beings with rights to their own thoughts and feelings. An accepting attitude means caring for people as vulnerable humans and suspending moral judgement on their goodness or badness. All helpers and clients are fallible human persons. The task of helping is to do just that: namely, help client to overcome skills weaknesses and develop skills strengths.

Below is a vignette in which many helping students were letting their own 'stuff' get in the way of how they perceived the client:

Students in a practicum class watched a video in which a middle-aged male talked about his anger, depression and isolation after the break-up of his marriage. On the surface, the client came over as an uptight, angry man with limited insight into both the consequences of the hostility with which he treated others and his choices in how to respond to them. The client had considered suicide and developed a suicide plan to make it easy for others to clean up the mess he would create by shooting himself. Throughout much of the video, some students ridiculed the client. When debriefed afterwards, they admitted difficulty with his attitudes towards women and said they would find it very hard to handle their feelings if someone like him came to them for help.

As helpers you need not only to be, but to be seen to be, psychologically present to clients. A major difference between advanced and less advanced helpers is that the latter accept clients and do not allow their vulnerability to obscure that of clients. Obnoxious client behaviours reveal pain and skills weaknesses. Such clients require your compassion and assistance rather than any negative personal reactions.

Numerous barriers may get in the way of an accepting attitude. You may become anxious when clients express certain feelings such as anger, depression or even joy. You may become anxious with certain categories of clients: for instance, people in authority or gay clients. Certain situations in helping may create anxiety: for instance, meeting new clients or recording sessions for supervision. Some helpers are prejudiced against clients such as migrants or the elderly. Beginning helpers may feel the need to present a professional facade that interferes with psychological presence. You may also be less accessible to clients if dealing with unfinished business from a previous encounter, tired or burned out. Sometimes physical factors, such as outside noise or heat, can interfere with the quality of your acceptance. You may be able to think of other barriers and filters applicable to you.

SKILL 3   SEND GOOD BODY MESSAGES

When listening and responding, helpers send messages to clients in three main ways: verbal, with words; vocal, with their voices; and nonverbal, with their body language. Here the focus is on body messages. Let us look at the body messages of two helpers:

Helper B (Bad)

Sits in a higher and more comfortable chair than the client. Communicates lack of interest in what clients say through bored facial expressions and through habits such as looking out of the window, finger drumming, poor eye contact, pulling lint off clothing and periodically glancing at the clock.

Helper G (Good)

Sits at same level as the client. Has an open and relaxed body posture. Has slight forward trunk lean. Gazes in the area of the client's face and maintains good eye contact. Uses head nods, facial expressions and gestures to show interest and understanding.

When clients talk, body messages are the main ways that helpers respond. Good body messages provide rewards to clients for talking. However, you need to be careful not to control your clients through selective use of body messages, for instance, showing interest when they discuss dreams and lack of interest when they are happy. When helpers talk, their body messages are important in supporting or negating what they say. Ideally, helpers communicate clearly with consistent verbal, voice and body messages. You are more likely to appear genuine if you send consistent messages.

SKILL 4   SEND GOOD VOICE MESSAGES

Beginning helpers need to develop an awareness of how they can use their voices as a tool for creating a safe emotional climate and showing understanding. Your voice communicates much about how anxious you are and how emotionally responsive you are to clients' feelings. Following are five dimensions of voice messages. They give the acronym VAPER – volume, articulation, pitch, emphasis and rate.

- *Volume.* Volume refers to loudness or quietness. How does your voice rate on a decibel meter? You need to respond at a level which is comfortable and easy to hear. Volume skills weaknesses include talking too loudly or softly, engaging in reciprocal mumbling with clients you perceive as vulnerable, and letting your voice trail away at the end of sentences.
- *Articulation.* Articulation refers to the distinctness and clarity of speech. Helpers need to enunciate their words clearly so that clients do not struggle to understand them.
- *Pitch.* Pitch refers to the height or depth of voice. An optimum pitch range includes all levels at which a pleasing voice can be produced without strain. Errors of pitch include being too high-pitched or too low-pitched.
- *Emphasis.* Emphasis means varying your voice appropriately to show understanding and maintain interest. Errors of emphasis include being monotonous, being melodramatic, and failing adequately to pick up clients' feelings and feeling nuances.
- *Rate.* Rate refers to how quickly or slowly you speak and to the frequency and duration of your pauses. Often speech rate is measured in words per minute, though an even more precise measure would be syllables per minute. Anxious helpers and clients tend to speak quickly. If you speak at a comfortable rate you may calm yourself down through placing less pressure on yourself than if speaking rapidly. Also, you may project a calmer image to your clients. Your use of silences can also enhance your rewarding listening. If you want to make it easier for clients to tell their stories, you can pause each time they stop speaking before responding, to see if they wish to continue.

SKILL 5   USE OPENERS, SMALL REWARDS AND OPEN-ENDED QUESTIONS

Using openers, small rewards and open-ended questions are three helper skills that make it easier for clients to talk.

Openers

Lifeskills helping always starts with encouraging clients to say why they have come. Openers, or permissions to talk, are brief statements indicating that helpers are in listening mode. They are door-openers that give clients the message, 'Please tell your story in your own words'. Examples of openers for use in initial helping sessions include:

Hello, I'm _____ . Please
    tell me why you've come?
    tell me what's concerning you?

If clients have been referred, you might say:

You've been referred by _____ . Now tell me how
you see your situation?

Sometimes helpers make opening statements in response to clients' body messages.

You seem very nervous.
You look upset.

Helpers working outside of formal helping settings may also use openers when they sense that people have personal agendas that they might want to share. Examples are:

Is there something on your mind?
I'm available if you want to talk.

Small rewards

Small rewards are brief verbal and nonverbal expressions designed to convey the message, 'I'm listening. Please continue'. Many small rewards are body messages, for instance, head nods. Following are some verbal small rewards, though perhaps 'Uh-hmm' is more a voice than a verbal message:

Uh-hmm	Sure	Indeed
Please continue	Tell me more	And
I hear you	Go on	Then

Another kind of small reward is to repeat the last word clients say:

Client to nurse

Client   I feel depressed.
Nurse   Depressed.

Open-ended questions

Open-ended questions allow clients to share their internal viewpoints without curtailing their options. Closed questions restrict how clients respond, and leading questions suggest how they should respond. Below is an example of each:

Client to student counsellor

Client	I've a new room mate.
Counsellor (open-ended question)	How to you feel about that?
Counsellor (closed question)	Is that good or bad?
Counsellor (leading question)	You should be pleased about that, shouldn't you?

SKILL 6   REWORD

The next three skills cluster around the theme of reflective responding. Empathy and active listening are alternative terms for reflective responding. Helpers move out of receiver mode and into sender mode to respond with understanding 'as if' in the clients' internal viewpoint. Reflective responding entails tuning into and 'mirroring' with your verbal, voice and body messages the crux of the meaning contained in your clients' verbal, voice and body messages. Reflective responses allow helpers to check whether they have accurately understood clients' messages. Initially, beginning helpers may find that reflective responding seems 'unnatural'. However, with practice and increased fluency, reflective responding can both appear and feel 'natural'. Following is an example of reflective responding:

Client to social worker

Client	I'm worried sick about making ends meet now that my husband's lost his job.
Social worker	You're extremely anxious about having enough money without your husband's income.

Apart from getting into your clients' frame of reference, the most basic skill in reflective responding is to reword or paraphrase rather than to parrot. Parrots are best kept in zoos or as pets – if you parrot clients, you will quickly lose them. Good rewordings of verbal content provide mirror reflections that clearly show your understanding, and start with the personal pronoun 'you' to indicate that you reflect clients' internal viewpoints. Following is an example of the difference between parroting and paraphrasing. How would you feel about each response if you were the client?

Client to personnel officer

Client	I've got mixed feelings about my job. I like the work, but I hate the people I work with.
Personnel officer (parroting)	You've got mixed feelings about your job. You like the work, but you hate the people you work with.
Personnel officer (paraphrasing)	You feel ambivalent about your work, being positive about what you do but very negative about your colleagues.

SKILL 7   REFLECT FEELINGS

Reflecting feelings is both similar to and different from rewording. The language of feelings is not words, because feelings are bodily sensations, which may then have word labels attached to them. Consequently, rewording alone has limitations. For example, clients may send voice and body messages that qualify or negate verbal messages – Angela says, 'I'm not angry with Bruce', both in a harsh voice and with glaring eyes. Sometimes both clients and helpers use the verb feel when they mean think. For instance, if Angela said, 'I feel he is no good', this statement would reflect more what she thought about Bruce than her angry feelings about him. This feel–think distinction is important not only when reflecting feelings, but when working with how clients think so as to influence how they feel.

Reflecting feelings involves both receiver and sender skills. *Receiver* skills include:

- understanding clients' face and body messages;
- understanding clients' voice messages;
- understanding clients' verbal messages;
- tuning into the flow of your own feelings about what clients communicate;
- taking into account the context of clients' messages;
- sensing both surface and underlying meanings of clients' messages.

Sender skills include:
- responding in ways that pick up clients' words and phrases for feelings;
- rewording feelings appropriately, using expressive rather than wooden language;
- using voice and body messages that neither add to nor subtract from the feelings conveyed;
- checking the accuracy of your understanding.

When reflecting feelings, you may wonder how best to respond to the numerous verbal, voice and body messages you have received. First, try to receive the messages accurately and decode the crux of what clients feel. Second, formulate and send emotionally expressive reflective responses that clearly communicate back to clients their core feelings. Following are some examples:

Client to counselling psychologist

Client   Each year around about now I feel depressed. I'm divorced and have no family of my own.

Christmas is a time for families and not for outsiders like me.

Psychologist You feel lonely and sad. Christmas is here again and you're on your own.

Client to marriage guidance counsellor

Client One moment she is all over me, the next moment she is mad. I just don't know where I stand.

Counsellor You're confused by getting mixed messages of affection and anger.

Patient to doctor

Patient My smoking is getting too expensive and dangerous.

Doctor It sounds as though you want to quit.

Sometimes helpers assist clients in finding right words for feelings. Here, reflecting feelings goes beyond rewording feelings to helping choose words for feelings that resonate for them.

Client to pastoral counsellor

Client I'm unsure how I feel about my father's death. I know I should be sad, but we had a difficult relationship. I have such conflicting feelings . . . sadness, yes, but there are others too . . .

Counsellor Relief, guilt, affection, anger . . . are any of these appropriate?

SKILL 8   REFLECT FEELINGS AND REASONS

A useful variation of reflective responding is to reflect both feelings and the reasons for them in a 'You feel . . . because . . .' format. The first advantages of this is that you place the reflection of the client's feeling at the start of your response. This way you access clients at a less intellectual level than if you go from thoughts to feelings. The second is that the format clearly distinguishes between the feeling or feelings and the thoughts contributing to them. You may add to clients' perceptions that you understand them if you show understanding of both feelings and their explanations rather than of feelings alone. Below is an example:

Youth to drug counsellor

Youth   I've struggled so hard to stay off drugs and now I'm afraid that with my girlfriend dumping me and my parents arguing all the time I will be forced back on to them.

Counsellor   *You feel* worried *because*, after all your efforts, you now are tempted to get back on drugs to deal with the pain you experience over losing your girlfriend and the bad atmosphere at home.

SKILL 9   AVOID UNREWARDING VERBAL 'DON'TS'

Clients require psychological safety and freedom to listen to, experience and explore themselves in helping. Furthermore, if they sense you are an unsafe person, they may fail to disclose or economize on disclosing significant information. Verbal responses that are likely to be 'don'ts' inside helping sessions include being judgemental; being patronizing; placing clients into superficial diagnostic categories; telling clients how they should feel, think and act; interrogating clients so that they feel they are being given the third degree; offering inappropriate explanations; and talking too much about yourself. Other unhelpful behaviours include unnecessarily reassuring clients and putting on a professional facade for your benefit rather than theirs.

SKILL 10   AVOID POOR THINKING SKILLS

The fact that you can bring good or poor thinking skills to helping has already been mentioned. All of the above verbal 'don'ts' reflect poor thinking skills. Through the way you think you can oppress rather than support clients. The need for effective thinking skills on the part of both helpers and clients pervades this book. Despite its importance and to avoid repetition, the topic is only mentioned in passing here.

ACTIVITIES

1. Think of at least two good and two poor listeners in your past or present life. What skills distinguish the good from the poor listeners?
2. Observe in your daily life how much you respond to others 'as if' in their internal viewpoints and how much they respond 'as if' in your internal viewpoint.
3. In what areas and ways might you experience difficulty in possessing an attitude of respect and acceptance towards clients?
4. Video-record yourself interviewing a 'client' and assess your body messages.
5. Audio-record yourself interviewing a 'client' and assess your voice messages.
6. Conduct a skills learning 'interview' with a partner in which, in the following order you:
   (a) parrot what he/she says;
   (b) paraphrase what he/she says;
   (c) reflect feelings; and
   (d) reflect feelings and reasons.
   Especially in the beginning, your partner should feed you relatively short sentences and then pause for your responses.
7. Put your rewarding listening skills together by interviewing a partner for 10 to 15 minutes. Playing back an audio-recording or video-recording may assist learning.

FIVE

How to identify and clarify problems

You're either part of the solution or part of the problem.
Eldridge Cleaver

In stage 1 of the lifeskills helping model, helpers move beyond developing rapport with clients to assist them in identifying and clarifying problems. Here helpers lay the foundation for how they later define these problems and intervene to develop clients' self-helping skills. Clients start telling their stories. Helpers try to make it easy for them not only to share their internal viewpoints, but to elaborate and expand on them. Within the context of supportive relationships, together helpers and clients look for additional information that pinpoints and illuminates main problem areas.

Helpers are companions, detectives and sniffer dogs. Helpers offer companionship to clients in the detective work of uncovering their problems and the reasons for them. A canine analogy is that of helpers assisting clients in 'sniffing around for bones' of relevant information. A common mistake of beginning helpers is to narrow the search too soon.

Many advantages flow from helpers and clients collaborating to identify and clarify problems. First, if treated as active partners, with little prompting most clients supply much information and many valuable insights. Second, if they have actively provided the information on which these are based, clients are more likely to accept subsequent redefinitions of problems in skills terms. Third, clients, are more likely to work on problems and skills weaknesss that they have played some part in discovering. Fourth, collaborating to understand clients' problems can develop the helping relationship more than rewarding listening alone. Helpers who work as active partners assisting clients in enlarging their understanding of problems may be perceived as more empathic than those staying solely within clients' internal viewpoints. The skills covered in this chapter assist clients in expanding their internal viewpoints through additional input from helpers' viewpoints.

STRUCTURING SKILLS

Structuring is a term used to describe the behaviours by which helpers let clients know how they work and their expectations about the client's role in the process. Clients may have prior knowledge about you through advertising, helping brochures and word of mouth. In addition, they may have spoken to you on the phone to set up the initial appointments. All of these contacts are important in establishing your helping credentials. Here my focus is on structuring at the start of and during initial sessions.

Following are some reasons, albeit overlapping, for structuring in initial sessions. First, helpers need to give clients permission to tell their stories. Second, clients may appreciate knowing the structure of the initial interview – what stages the helper intends working through. Third, clients may wish to know the framework within which the helper works.

Below are some examples of what you might say when you meet a client for the first time:

Permission to talk

You   Hello, Bruce, my name is Cynthia Ashton. We have about 40 minutes and everything you say is confidential. Please tell me why you've come.

Permission to talk plus outlining initial session structure

You   Hello, Bruce, my name is Cynthia Ashton. We have about 40 minutes and everything you say is confidential. I suggest we proceed as follows. First, you explain what brings you here. Then together we explore your problem or problems in more detail to understand them better. Then, depending on what we find, I may suggest some ways you may think and act differently to help you cope better. Once we agree on what skills might be useful, then we can look at ways to develop them. So, please tell me what's concerning you.

Permission to talk, initial session structure plus lifeskills helping framework

You   Hello, Bruce, my name is Cynthia Ashton. We have about 40 minutes and everything you say is confidential. I work within the lifeskills helping framework. This educational approach assumes that people usually sustain problems by learned ways in which they think and act – what are sometimes called, without any moral judgement, thinking-skills weaknesses and action-skills weaknesses. My role is to help you to describe your problems more fully and look for the skills you need to manage them better. Once we agree on what these skills are, we can discuss some ways you can learn to develop them. During this session we will complete as many of these tasks as we can. Do you have any questions?

If anything, when starting sessions I prefer to structure by briefly asking clients to say why they have come. By finding out 'where clients are at' and making emotional contact with them you show empathy for their needs and anxieties about sharing problems. Later, you can provide initial session structure and information about the lifeskills helping approach. For instance, an appropriate time might be *after* clients have had an initial opportunity to tell their stories and *before* you have assisted them in clarifying their problems more fully.

How you send voice and body messages is important when you structure. Your voice messages should indicate your commitment to what you do. Good voice-message skills include easy audibility, comfortable speech rate, firm voice, clear articulation and appropriate variations in emphasis. Your body messages should support your verbal and voice messages, for example, by relaxed body posture and appropriate use of gesture, gaze and eye contact.

QUESTIONING SKILLS

In stage 1 of the lifeskills helping model, helpers ask questions that enable clients to describe their internal viewpoints more fully; but questioning can definitely be overdone. For instance, after initial structuring, helpers can encourage clients to tell their stories in their own words and at their own pace rather than control through questions what they talk about. Early in initial sessions you can ask either open-ended questions that do not restrict how clients respond, or questions that directly follow on from what they say. Also, before asking another question, you can reflect clients' answers, especially their feelings, and pause to see if they want to go on. By avoiding interrogating clients, you take the pressure off both them and yourself.

Below is an example of a counsellor giving a new client the 'third degree'.

School counsellor	Please tell me why you've come?
Pupil	I'm angry with my father.
School counsellor	Why are you angry with your father?
Pupil	Because he is always shouting at me.
School counsellor	Why is he always shouting at you?
Pupil	Because he does not like how I behave.
School counsellor	Why doesn't he like how you behave?

Here is a gentler approach to assisting the client to talk about his problem. Note how the counsellor picks up how the client feels. Clients need understanding as human beings, not just intellectual analysis of their problems. Also, the counsellor assists the client to elaborate his internal viewpoint rather than to supply information wanted for external reasons:

School counsellor	Please tell me why you've come?
Pupil	I'm angry with my father.
School counsellor	Angry with Dad. Go on.
Pupil	He is always shouting at me and last week he hit me.
School counsellor	You sound even more mad at him now he's hit you.

| Pupil | That's right. I'd really like to leave home, but haven't got the money. |
| **School counsellor** | So you're desperate to the point of wanting to move out. Would you tell me more about your situation? |

Why ask questions rather than just reflect what clients say? First, questions can show that helpers are interested in clients' experiences. Second, skilled questioning can assist clients in identifying their real areas of concern. Clients may come to helping with 'calling cards' – problems that are easier for them discuss than the problems they really want to discuss. For example, parents may find it easier to discuss problem children rather than their distressed marriages. Good use of questions can accelerate their willingness to become more open. Third, questions can help break down clients' problems into their component parts. For example, Mary Rogers, a 19-year-old college student, says that life is hardly worth living. By using questions, the helper not only assess how depressed and anxious Mary is, but locates areas in which Mary may have skills weaknesses that contribute to her negative feelings about herself and life. Sub-areas of Mary's overall problem include a poor relationship with her depressed mother, difficulty in making lasting friendships, doubts about her sexual adequacy, anxiety attacks in crowded places, few recreational outlets and poor study habits. Fourth, questions can assist clients to access material that lies below the surface, but is not unconscious. Fifth, questions can assist helpers in exploring hypotheses about clients' thinking- and action-skills weaknesses in each problem area.

Areas for questions

Following are some of the main areas in which helpers ask questions to clarify clients' problems:

- *Basic details.* Basic details about problems include onset, frequency, intensity, past experiences, current situation, precipitating causes and consequences.
- *Feelings.* What emotions are associated with problems – for instance, anxiety or sadness – and how severe are they?

- *Physical reactions.* What physical reactions are associated with problems – for instance, knotted stomach or sweaty palms – and how severe are they?
- *Thoughts and personal meanings.* What thoughts precede, accompany and follow problems? What are the personal meanings of problems to clients?
- *Actions.* How do clients actually behave in the problem areas? What verbal, voice and body messages do they and any significant others send?
- *Coping strategies.* How have clients attempted to cope with their problems to date? What strengths and supports do they have?

Helpers have numerous other questioning choices. Always, you require sensitivity to the timing and intimacy level of questions. Also, consider how many topics to cover and in how much detail. For example, if you focus tightly on problems stated first, you may block clients from revealing others.

Types of questions

Helpers also need to choose among different types of questions, including the following:

- *Open-ended versus closed questions.* Open-ended questions give clients considerable choice in how to respond, whereas closed questions restrict choice. An open-ended question is, 'How do you experience your marriage?'; a closed question is 'Is your marriage good or bad?' Leading questions are even more restricted versions of closed questions, since they suggest one answer only, for example, 'You feel pretty angry with your parents, don't you?' When working with new clients, many helpers start by using open-ended questions until they understand clients better.
- *Specific detail questions.* Aim to collect descriptive information not only about problems but about clients' thoughts, feelings, physical reactions and actions relating to them. Specific detail questions include 'How frequent is it?' and 'How did you actually behave?' 'Show me' questions are good for eliciting specific details about voice and body messages, for instance, 'Imagine that I am your . . . . Show me how you actually spoke to me.' Request-for-example

questions, such as 'Tell me of a specific instance', can also illuminate details of problems.

- *Elaboration questions.* These are open questions that give clients opportunities to expand on what they say. Illustrative elaboration questions are 'Would you care to elaborate?' and 'Is there anything more you wish to add?'
- *Clarification questions.* These seek information about and clarify your perceptions of clients' words and phrases. Examples include, 'When you say . . ., what do you mean?' and 'Sounds to me you're saying . . .'.
- *Challenging questions.* These confront clients with the need to produce evidence for their perceptions, for instance, 'Where is the evidence for . . .?'
- *Personal-meanings questions.* These elicit the personal or symbolic meanings that problems or aspects of problems have for clients, for instance, 'What is the meaning of all this for you?' Helpers sometimes use such questions to focus clients back on themselves rather than externalize about others. Helpers can also ask cultural-meaning questions, for instance, 'What's the meaning of that behaviour in your culture?'

How to question

In lifeskills helping, questions provide information as much for clients as for helpers. Helpers should always work in partnership with clients. By asking too many questions, many beginning helpers put themselves in the vulnerable position of experts who are then unable to deliver solutions. Always ask questions with a purpose and not for questioning's sake. Avoid 'jack-rabbiting', in which you hop quickly from one topic to another. Frequently, your next questions can encourage clients to build upon their previous responses. Soften your questioning by interspersing reflective responding. If you provide good emotional climates, clients do much of the work for you; however, if you provide poor emotional climates, clients clam up. You may use pauses and silences to encourage clients to engage in self-exploration and to move beyond superficial answers.

How you question is very important. Be sensitive to clients' anxieties and vulnerabilities, and use tact both in asking questions and in responding to answers. Monitor your voice and body messages – for instance, clients may feel overwhelmed if your voice is loud and harsh, and if you use poor gaze and eye contact they may resist answering your questions. Last, but not least, carefully observe how clients answer questions. Clients convey much information by what they omit to say or only partially say and by their voice and body messages.

SUMMARIZING SKILLS

Helper summaries are brief statements that pull together the various parts of what clients communicate. Sometimes helpers can ask clients to summarize. Summaries can be useful in all stages of the lifeskills helping model, but here the focus is on helper summaries in initial sessions. Such summaries have numerous purposes, including ensuring that you understand clients, showing understanding, rewarding clients for talking, establishing your presence with clients who talk a lot, and acting as bridging statements between parts of a session. How you provide summaries is important, along with what you say. For instance, having a relaxed body posture and using a measured speech rate may help calm down anxious clients; however, if you look tense and match their rapid speech rate, you collude in maintaining their anxiety. Following are some different types of summaries you might use when identifying and clarifying problems.

Basic reflective summary

Basic reflective summaries mirror the main feelings and content of what clients say. For instance, when clients respond to your request to say why they have come, you may choose not to interrupt them for a time and then summarize what they have said to date. Your reflective summary enables the clients to continue with their current train of thought or move on to another topic. As with reflecting shorter excerpts of what clients say, often it helps clients to feel understood if you reflect their core feelings at the start of your summaries:

Helper
You're scared and unhappy that Mum and Dad fight so much. You think they may break up. They have less time and energy to spend with you and Maggie. Home isn't the fun place it used to be.

A variation of the basic reflective summary is to use the 'You feel . . . because . . .' format. For instance, the above client, Timmy, *feels* scared and unhappy *because* he thinks that Mum and Dad fight so much that they may break up and that home is no longer a fun place to be. An advantage of the 'You feel . . . because . . .' format is that it distinguishes between feelings and the thoughts and perceptions contributing to them.

Identification-of-problem-areas summary

Imagine a client comes to helping and starts describing a number of different problems. Summaries that identify the different problem areas mentioned can provide clients with clearer and more succinct statements than those they managed on their own. Such summaries can also break down larger problems into their component parts, and can provide a basis for asking clients to give priority to the problems that are most important or that they want to work on first:

> **Helper**
> You started by talking about how much you disliked men making sexual innuendos and touching you without permission. You then moved on to discuss your problems with your boyfriend whom you think is beginning to take you for granted. You then raised the issue of whether you should move out of home and establish your independence. Which of these issues would you like to focus on first?

Details-of-problem summary

In initial sessions, helpers work with clients to describe problems more fully. For instance, clients who say they are shy may react differently according to how well they know people, to different kinds of people, in different situations and so on. Numerous different possibilities require checking to arrive at accurate descriptive definitions. Helpers need to avoid making erroneous assumptions about details of clients' problems until they are told. You may take notes to assist your memory. Furthermore, later you may collect more descriptive information.

Helper
We've now spent some time exploring the details of your statistics anxiety problem and I'd like to check with you that I've understood the main points. You are aged 31 and returned to university to do a psychology degree. You enjoy the people part of the course, but hate the numerical part. It is now six weeks into your first year and you are considering giving up the course because you think 'I just can't do statistics.' You have always had a mental block over maths and avoided the subject as much as you could. You get tense when you sit in statistics lectures, your heart pounds and you find it difficult to concentrate. You have started to avoid doing the assignments and this makes it even harder for you to understand the lectures. You are increasingly worried about having to sit your statistics exam at the end of term and wake up in the night thinking about it. You enjoy all other aspects of the course, and your feedback so far has been very good. You have spoken neither to your lecturer nor to your tutor about your statistics problem. You feel isolated from the other students on account of your age and do not like the thought of younger people understanding statistics when you don't. Is there anything important that I've left out?

By means of details-of-problems summaries, helpers may make the transition from stage 1 of the lifeskills helping model, focused on identifying and clarifying problems, to stage 2, focused on assisting problems and redefining them in skills terms.

Helpers use summarizing not only during, but at the beginning and end of sessions. Some helpers end sessions by reviewing what they and clients have achieved. Such summaries can include an overview of homework. Helpers may summarize the previous session at the start of the next one. However, allow space for clients to mention any pressing current concerns.

CONFRONTING SKILLS

Helpers may use confronting or challenging skills to assist clients in clarifying problems. The purpose of confronting is to challenge clients' existing perceptions so that you can both work with more and better information. Ideally, confrontations are invitations for exploration that stimulate clients to think more deeply and to provide additional information about problems and problematic skills.

What to confront

Helpers can use confronting skills to challenge inconsistencies, possible distortions of reality and inadequate acknowledgement of choice.

- *Confronting inconsistencies.* You may experience inconsistencies in messages your clients send. A common helper response when confronting inconsistencies is, 'On the one hand you say . . . but on the other hand . . .', for example, 'On the one hand you say you are sorry about what you did, but on the other hand you smile when you recount the look on her face.' This way of confronting is often shortened to, 'You say . . . but . . .', for example, 'You say you are sorry, but you smile when you recount the look on her face.'
- *Confronting possible distortions of reality.* Clients' perceptions are of varying degrees of accuracy. For example, James, a 43-year-old bank manager, says 'I am no good at public speaking'; Monica, a 36-year-old single parent, says 'My children never do anything around the house'; and Karl, a 29-year-old factory foreman, says 'My workers are all against me.' Sometimes helpers need either to challenge clients' perceptions directly or to invite them to provide evidence to support their version of reality. A good way of confronting possible distortions of reality is, 'You say . . ., but where's the evidence?'. In the above examples, helpers might ask James, Monica and Karl to provide evidence that he was no good at public speaking, her children never did anything around the house, or his workers were all against him, respectively. In this way helpers invite clients to provide their own evidence to negate or confirm their perceptions. If clients still have difficulty challenging their perceptions, helpers can ask questions that might elicit different evidence, for instance, James might be asked if he had any strengths as a public speaker, Monica to think of occasions when her children did some housework, and Karl for instances of workers being positive to him. Always remember that clients' perceptions are their subjective reality and that their perceptions may be justified.

- *Confronting not acknowledging choice.* Lifeskills helping heavily emphasizes personal responsibility. You can confront clients with their role as choosers in their lives. For example, if clients say, 'I *can't* do that', you might ask, 'Can you say "I *won't* do that"?' Another example is that of challenging a teacher who thinks he or she must always agree with his or her headteacher to acknowledge he or she can choose whether or not to agree.

How to confront

Following are some guidelines on how to confront:

1. *Start with reflective responding.* If they think you understand their internal viewpoint, clients are more likely to listen to challenges from your external viewpoint.
2. *Where possible, help clients to confront themselves.* Often, assisting clients in self-confrontation leads to less resistance than directly confronting them from your external viewpoint.
3. *Do not talk down.* Keep your confrontations at a democratic level to avoid clients perceiving them as 'put-downs'.
4. *Use a minimum amount of 'muscle'.* Only confront as strongly as your goal requires. Strong confrontations, though sometimes desirable, are best avoided in initial sessions since trust is not yet established.
5. *Use good voice and body messages.* Your voice and body messages should show respect for clients and support your verbal messages. For example, look at clients when confronting them, and avoid threatening voice and body messages, such as shouting or finger pointing.
6. *Leave the ultimate responsibility with clients.* Allow clients to decide whether your confrontations actually assist them in moving forward to explore and understand their problems.
7. *Do not overdo it.* Nobody likes being persistently challenged. With constant confrontations you create unsafe emotional climates.

FURTHER SKILLS

In addition to the skills already described, following are some further skills for identifying and clarifying problems.

Self-disclosing skills

Helper self-disclosure relates to the way you let yourself be known to clients. Showing involvement and disclosing personal information are two major ways of disclosing. Self-involving disclosures, for instance, 'I admire your courage', can personalize the helping process. In particular, self-involving disclosures expressing positive rather than negative feelings about clients draw favourable reactions. Disclosing personal information and experiences may help clients feel you understand what they go through, for example, sharing experiences of unemployment, parenting and drug addiction. However, proceed with caution, since you may focus helping on yourself rather than on your clients.

Understanding-context skills

Problems and problematic skills do not exist in vacuums. Helpers require skills of eliciting information about and understanding the contexts of problems. For example, relevant contexts within which to understand specific problems include clients' religion, culture, race, social class, health and sexual orientation. Showing genuine knowledge about different contexts, acknowledging helper–client differences and encouraging clients to discuss problems in terms of broader contexts can be useful helper skills.

Managing-initial-resistance skills

Resistance may be broadly defined as anything that gets in the way of helping. At best, most clients are ambivalent when coming to helping. At the same time as wanting to change, they may have anxieties both about the processes and consequences of change. Other clients reluctantly come to helping, for example, pupils sent by teachers to school counsellors for 'straightening out'. Using rewarding listening skills that show clients you understand their internal viewpoints may diminish resistances. Other strategies include giving clients permission to discuss their reluctance and fears about helping, and enlisting client self-interest, for example, by questions like, 'What are your goals in the situation?', and 'How is your current behaviour helping you?'. Helpers need to be sensitive to the pace at which different clients can work, since clients feeling pressured by helpers may become even more resistant.

ACTIVITIES

1. Either on your own or with a partner, practise each of the following ways of structuring at the start of an initial session: permission to talk; permission to talk plus outlining initial session structure; and permission to talk, initial session structure plus lifeskills helping framework.
2. Either on your own or with a partner, practise each of the following questioning skills: asking open-ended, specific detail, elaboration, clarification, challenging and personal-meanings questions.
3. Either on your own or with a partner, practise each of the following summarizing skills: basic reflective summary, identification-of-problem-areas summary, and details-of-problem summary.
4. Either on your own or with a partner, practise each of the following kinds of confronting skills: confronting inconsistencies, confronting possible distortions of reality, and confronting not acknowledging choice.
5. Work with a partner and conduct an initial session in which you assist your client to identify and clarify a problem. Use rewarding listening skills plus structuring, questioning, summarizing and confronting skills.
   Afterwards, discuss and reverse roles.

SIX

How to assess feelings

*No emotion, any more than a wave, can long retain
its own individual form.*
Henry Ward Beecher

The next four chapters present skills for stage 2 of the lifeskills helping model: assess problem(s) and redefine in skills terms (see Figure 6.1). This and the subsequent two chapters focus on how to assess feelings,

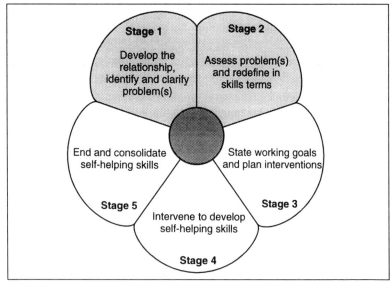

Figure 6.1 *Stage 2 Assess problem(s) and redefine in skills terms*

thinking and acting, respectively. Chapter 9 reviews skills of redefining problems in skills terms.

Both helpers and clients engage in assessment throughout the lifeskills helping model, including when clients work on maintaining and developing skills afterwards. However, whereas developing helping relationships and obtaining descriptive information are the main tasks of stage 1, assessing clients' problems more thoroughly and forming hypotheses about how they are sustained are central to stage 2. Together, helpers and clients reform descriptive definitions of problems into skills redefinitions that pinpoint how clients think and act in ways that sustain problems.

Following are examples of clients' statements of feelings:

'I get nervous at interviews.'
'I feel empty and that my life has no meaning.'
'I feel lonely and isolated.'
'I feel guilty when I get angry.'

Lifeskills helpers need to be keenly attuned to how well clients function as feelings persons. You need to assess clients' feelings for numerous reasons. First, you have an ethical duty to protect clients and need to be sensitive to whether they are suicide risks. Second, you need to be aware of whether clients require referral to psychiatrists, for instance, schizophrenic or manic-depressive clients. Third, you need the ability to evaluate clients' emotional responsiveness. Since clients often come with previous experiences of their feelings going unheard, they require assistance in experiencing, acknowledging and understanding their feelings. Clients badly out of touch with their feelings may require longer-term help.

Paying close attention to feelings may enable you to clarify what clients' real agendas are. For instance, a client's 'calling card' may be a work-stress problem, but you may infer from feelings clues that a domestic relationship problem is the real agenda. Frequently, clients' disproportionate or inappropriate feelings can provide avenues for exploring possible thinking-skills and action-skills weaknesses. A further reason for assessing clients' feelings is that you can assist them in developing skills for assessing their own feelings both during and after helping.

WHAT TO ASSESS

In Chapter 4, I reviewed the listening skills of identifying and reflecting feelings. Here I review dimensions of feelings from the viewpoint of assessing problems:

- *Capacity to experience feelings.* Some clients lack emotional responsiveness across a wide range of feelings; their emotions are flat and lifeless. Other clients have difficulty experiencing specific feelings, for example, anger, sexual attraction or affection. Some clients mask their difficulties in experiencing their feelings by exaggerating them, and many clients have difficulty getting in touch with their real wants and wishes. Sometimes difficulty experiencing feelings may be compounded by difficulty in communicating feelings to others.
- *Energy level.* How much energy do clients possess? How much vitality and zest for life do they have? Clients' energy levels can be influenced by anxiety, depression and relationship conflicts. Since medical explanations for low energy exist, referral to doctors for medical checks may be advisable.
- *Self-esteem.* How confident are clients? To what extent are their levels of self-esteem pervasive, or do they fluctuate across different situations? Clients' negative views of themselves can contribute to feelings of anxiety, depression, apathy, loneliness and anger, among others. Clients with badly damaged self-esteem may be candidates for longer-term helping. Clients with reasonable self-esteem possess a useful asset for working on problems and problematic skills.
- *Anxiety and defensiveness.* Unhelpful or debilitating anxiety reflects an exaggerated sense of danger and may be a pervasive trait or a state attached to specific situations. Many beginning helpers pay insufficient attention to assessing clients' areas and levels of anxiety. A distinguishing characteristic of skilled helpers is their canine ability to 'sniff out' clients' anxieties tactfully and understand their significance. Such helpers are also keenly attuned to the less obvious ways in which clients use defensive processes or security operations – for instance, denial or projection – to contain and manage anxiety. Anxiety on the part of both clients and helpers is always present in helping interviews. Pay attention to how both your own and your

clients' anxieties can interfere with the helping process.

- *Physical reactions.* Physical reactions both represent and accompany feelings. For instance, physical reactions associated with anxiety include heart throbbing, dry mouth, butterflies in the stomach, shaking, feeling faint, sweaty palms, lowered sex urge, period problems and sleep difficulties, among others. Clients may misperceive their physical reactions in ways that contribute to their distress, for instance, shy clients perceiving their blushing to be far more obvious than it is. Clients can also react to their physical reactions in unhelpful ways, for instance, feeling tense and anxious and using this as a sign to feel even more tense and anxious, even to the extent of a full-blown panic attack.

- *Psychophysiologic disorders.* Psychophysiologic or psychosomatic disorders are caused and maintained primarily by psychological and emotional rather than physical or organic factors. Psychophysiologic disorders can affect the skin – for instance, acne – and the body's musculoskeletal, respiratory, cardiovascular, blood and lymphatic, gastrointestinal and endocrine systems. The more common psychophysiologic disorders include peptic ulcers, migraine headaches, asthma and high blood pressure.

- *Feelings about helping and the helper.* Be sensitive to clients' feelings and expectations regarding helping. For example, they may dislike being in the client role or may want to become dependent on you, and they may have a range of feelings about you on such dimensions as like/dislike and trust/mistrust. Often clients' feelings about helpers reflect their earlier learning histories, for instance, sensitivity to cues of liking or rejection stemming from earlier negative experiences. The 'bottom line' is that clients require a minimum level of positive feelings towards you to continue working with you.

When assessing feelings, helpers need to attend to their strength and persistence. Often feeling intensity is described by words such as 'mild', 'moderate' or 'severe'. For example, clients may be mildly, moderately or severely depressed, though perceptions may differ as to what is mild, moderate or severe. Persistence of feelings may be described by words like 'long-standing', 'chronic' or 'acute'. Chronic anxiety means persistent anxiety, whereas acute anxiety implies one or more sharp and short episodes.

Helpers and clients have the task of assessing appropriateness of feelings. For instance, what are appropriate feelings of grief, guilt, anger, sadness, shyness and anxiety? When you assess appropriateness of feelings, consider clients' unique styles of expressing and reporting feelings as well as a host of situational, contextual and cultural factors. A question in assessing the appropriateness of feelings is their positive or negative consequences for clients and others. Feelings may also be assessed in terms of psychiatric classification. Always take into account the effects of any medication clients are using.

HOW TO ASSESS

From the moment of first contact, helpers need to tune in to how clients feel. The more you can show sensitivity to clients' feelings, the more they are likely to experience, disclose and explore them with you of their own accord. Below are some skills useful for eliciting and assessing how clients feel.

Be a rewarding listener

Rewarding listening provides safe emotional climates for clients to experience and share their feelings. You require good skills at picking up both feelings and feelings nuances. Receiver skills include paying close attention to verbal, voice and body messages and inconsistencies between them. Listen not only for what is said, but for what is only partially said or left unsaid. For instance, clients who describe angry feelings may find it harder to acknowledge and share feelings of hurt. Clients differ in how clearly they send voice and body messages, and both consciously and intuitively skilled helpers listen 'with the third ear' and observe 'with the third eye' for omissions, discrepancies and glimpses of feelings that are clues to underlying and, as yet, unshared feelings. A good way to sense the realness of what clients describe is to be open to your own experiencing of both how and what they communicate. Your feelings are a clue to assessing their feelings.

Sender skills for helping clients share feelings include good attending behaviour, accurate reflections, and offering sensitive and supportive companionship as clients explore emerging feelings and reasons for them. Always be mindful of the pace at which clients prefer to work. Undue pressure can contribute to resistances; however, encouragement can assist clients in experiencing and disclosing feelings, for example, comments like:

'You seem on the verge of sharing something. Just take your time.'
'You're close to tears. It's okay to cry. There's a box of tissues if you need them.'

Especially as you come to know clients better, you can use advanced reflections of feelings to assist them to articulate more personally relevant, emotionally tinged and anxiety-evoking feelings. Such advanced reflections attempt to identify underlying agendas and themes. Since you are sharing 'hunches' made from inferences, you require tact and humility. You also need to perceive accurately how clients respond. For example, the helper below gets the impression that a single mother talks around rather than admits her feelings that she would much rather her 19-year-old daughter Fran left home.

Helper
You've made a number of comments critical of Fran and how she expects you to look after her. You have also expressed a desire to get back in control of your life. You seem to be saying you want Fran to move out.

Use focusing-on-feelings questions

Helpers may use focusing-on-feelings questions to elicit, identify, clarify and encourage clients to explore feelings and physical reactions. Generally, you should intersperse reflective responses with questions, perhaps especially so when assisting clients to move from 'head space' to 'heart space'. You may ask questions to elicit both there-and-then and here-and-now feelings. An example of a question focused on the there-and-then is, 'And how did you feel when that happened?'. A question focused on the here-and-now is, 'How do you feel talking about it now?'

Often, rather than assuming you understand, you need to clarify what clients mean when they use feelings words. For instance, you might ask, 'When you say you get very anxious, what exactly do you mean?', or 'When you say you get very anxious, what are your specific feelings and physical reactions?' Then you assist clients in pinpointing specific feelings and physical reactions.

Helpers can assist clients in elaborating on how they feel. For instance, you may ask open-ended questions like, 'Describe the feeling more fully'. Then you may ask follow-up questions that encourage clients to expand on their responses, for example, 'You say you feel weepy. Can you describe the feeling more fully?' Additional clarifying feelings questions helpers may ask include:

'Describe how your body experiences the feeling.'
'Do you have any visual images that accompany the feeling?'
'Are there any other feelings that accompany that feeling?'
'When do you start experiencing these feelings?'
'How persistent and intense is the feeling?'

Use visualizing and role play

You may need to use emotion-eliciting techniques. Using visualizing and role play are two skills by which helpers can assist clients in experiencing and describing feelings more fully. Clients can be asked to shut their eyes and visualize a particular scene, past or future, and describe the emotions elicitied by it. Remember that clients differ in their visualizing abilities. Alternatively, helpers may role-play scenes with clients – for instance, a playground argument with another child – and process the emotions elicited by them. You may need to encourage clients to do role plays with you.

Use feelings-monitoring logs and questionnaires

Helpers can encourage clients to become more aware of how they feel without necessarily using monitoring logs. Daily rating forms and specific incident logs are two ways in which clients can monitor their feelings. An example of a daily rating form is to ask clients to rate their pain on a scale ranging from 0 (no pain at all) to 9 (excruciating pain). Specific incident logs can be targeted on feelings, such as anger or shyness, and on different temptations, for instance, drinking or drug-taking. Figure 6.2 shows a possible format for a specific incident log.

Date and time	What happened (Situation)	My feelings and physical reactions

Figure 6.2   *A specific incident log*

Helpers can use questionnaires to assess feelings, such as anxiety, depression, mood states and specific fears. These may, though, be unnecessary for many clients, especially in brief helping.

FORM FEELINGS HYPOTHESES

When assessing feelings, helpers form hypotheses both to guide collection of information and also to draw conclusions. Such feelings hypotheses are open to modification as helping progresses,. By the end of the first session, skilled helpers are likely to have formed hypotheses in each of the following areas of clients' feelings: capacity to experience feelings, energy level, self-esteem, anxiety and defensiveness, physical reactions, psychophysiological disorders, and feelings about helping and the helper. Experienced helpers may not verbalize all such hypotheses, even to themselves. Nevertheless, it is unlikely that they will have overlooked any of these feelings areas.

ACTIVITIES

1. Briefly explain how important you consider it is in initial sessions to assess each of the following dimensions of clients' feelings:
   capacity to experience feelings;
   energy level;
   self-esteem;
   anxiety and defensiveness;
   physical reactions;
   psychophysiological disorders;
   feelings about helping and the helper.
2. Give your reactions to each of the following ways of assessing clients' feelings in initial sessions:

      rewarding listening;
      focusing-on-feelings questions;
      using visualizing;
      using role play;
      feelings-monitoring logs;
      questionnaires.

3. Conduct an interview with a partner in which you use some of the assessing-feelings skills listed in activity 2 to form hypotheses about each of the feelings areas listed in activity 1. Afterwards, discuss your hypotheses and reverse roles.

SEVEN

How to assess thinking skills

*The highest possible stage in moral culture is when
we recognize that we ought to control our thoughts.*
Charles Darwin

Clients, like all humans, are prone to 'stinkin' thinkin''. People
support themselves with thinking-skills strengths: they oppress
themselves with thinking-skills weaknesses. It is important that you
assess and help clients to assess how they think. The lifeskills helping
approach assumes that all clients have one or more thinking-skills
weaknesses that sustains each presenting problem. Often, when
clients have many problems, the same thinking-skills weaknesses
recur. Many beginning helpers have limited experience in thinking
about how they think. A good way to become more proficient at
thinking about how clients think is to develop your skills of thinking
about how you think.

WHAT TO ASSESS

Following are some thinking-skills that you can assess. Remember to
observe strengths as well as weaknesses. When learning how to assess
thinking, you may start by focusing on just one or two client thinking-
skills areas until you become better at it. I review interventions for
developing clients' thinking skills in Chapter 13.

Owning responsibility for choosing

Many clients have a diminished sense that they are always choosers, so that in differing degrees they sacrifice their ability to create their lives. For various reasons, they remain unaware or insufficiently aware that they have choices in how they feel, think and act. Such clients may need to become more aware that they can become the architects, authors or builders of their lives. To the extent that they have been 'condemned' to freedom, they have also been condemned to the responsibility to fashion their lives out of that freedom. The lifeskills approach assumes that, despite adverse circumstances, clients are always personally responsible for their choices. They may need assistance to develop skills of assuming more effective responsibility for these, but that does not negate their underlying responsibility to choose.

Using coping self-talk

Here self-talk refers to what clients say to themselves before, during and after specific situations. Look for negative self-talk that contributes to self-defeating feelings and actions. Following is an example of how Rosalie uses negative self-talk to disturb herself prior to giving a talk in public:

> I'm no good at public speaking. I know I should be better, but every time I seem to mess things up. I feel nervous and then everybody sees me shaking and blushing. They all seem to be looking at me.

The way Rosalie talks greatly increases her chances of being highly anxious and performing poorly. Her self-talk indicates she is overly self-conscious about what others think. She needs to develop skills of talking to herself in ways that calm her down – for instance, 'Relax' – and that coach her through what she needs to do – for instance, 'Look at the audience.' Also, she requires skills of telling herself about her realistic assets rather than putting herself down with over-generalizations like, 'I'm no good at public speaking.'

Choosing realistic personal rules

Personal rules or beliefs are the dos and don'ts by which people live. They can be realistic or unrealistic, rational or irrational. Albert Ellis has coined the term 'mustabation' to refer to rigid personal rules characterized by 'musts', 'oughts' and 'shoulds'. Targets for unrealistic personal rules can be: (1) clients themselves, for instance, 'I must always gain everyone's approval'; (2) other people, for instance, 'Others must always consider my feelings'; and (3) clients' environments, for instance, 'Life must always be fair.' Apart from mustabatory language, characteristics of unrealistic personal rules include making demands rather than stating preferences, expecting perfection, rating yourself as well as your specific characteristics negatively, and engaging in catastrophic fantasies about the negative consequences of not attaining your rules. Unrealistic rules can lead to self-defeating feelings and actions. For instance, underlying some of Rosalie's negative self-talk about public speaking may be unrealistic rules such as, 'I must give the perfect talk', and 'I must be approved of by everyone.' Such rules contribute to heightened anxiety and lowered performance.

Choosing to perceive accurately

A Chinese proverb states, 'Two-thirds of what we see is behind our eyes.' Clients relate to themselves and each other in terms of working models, and are often much too hard on themselves, exaggerating negatives and ignoring or minimizing positives. For instance, Rosalie was choosing to perceive her public speaking skills negatively rather than trying to identify some strengths or potential strengths. However, in relationship conflicts, clients may be too easy on themselves – their partners are black and they are white. In varying degrees, clients may distort or deny incoming information that contradicts their models of self and others. Such defensive-process or security operations enable them to maintain consistency at the expense of reality. Errors in how clients perceive include:

- tunnel vision, in which they ignore many salient factors in situations;
- polarized thinking, where they think in black-and-white terms;

- over-generalizing, where broader inferences are inadequately supported by available facts;
- specific defences such as projection (seeing their own defects in others).

Attributing cause accurately

Clients commonly attribute cause from outside to inside, thus maintaining their 'stuckness' and seeing, for instance, their anger, anxiety, depression, guilt as the result of others' rather than their own choices. For example, David justifies striking his wife because her behaviour 'made him do it', but in reality, David chooses to allow his own behaviour to be controlled by his wife's behaviour rather than attributing the cause of his violence to himself. Sometimes, people attribute too much responsibility to themselves, for instance, unemployed people may misperceive the contribution of broader economic forces to their job loss. In short, you need to observe the extent to which clients externalize or internalize rather than appropriately assign the causes of what happens, both within specific situations and across situations.

Predicting realistically

Humans lead their lives into the future, so to live is to predict; but predictions can be of varying degrees of accuracy. Many clients' predictions have a heightened sense of danger that contributes to anxiety – to put it another way, they overestimate possible risks or negative consequences, and at the same time, when contemplating action, may either fail to identify possible rewards or not give them sufficient weight. Other clients underestimate risks, for instance, gamblers, heavy smokers, those engaging in unsafe sex, and manic business speculators with grandiose schemes. Some of these clients also overestimate the rewards or positive consequences of their actions. Predicting realistically entails making accurate inferences of risk and reward on the basis of available facts. Some clients need to think less egocentrically, that is, before acting they need to become more aware of and predict more realistically the effect of their behaviour on others.

Setting realistic goals

Poor goal-setting skills contribute to some clients experiencing difficulty in assuming effective responsibility for their lives. Sometimes poor goal-setting skills are indicative of deeper insecurities; on other occasions, they may be skills weaknesses in their own right. Goals can be immediate, short-term, medium-term or long-term. They may be set in any areas of clients' lives, such as relationships, health, finances, work, study or leisure, to mention but some. In relationships, goals frequently need to be negotiated so that they become shared goals. Errors in goal setting include not reflecting values, insufficient realism, inadequate specificity and unclear time frames. Also, clients may fail to think in skills terms when setting goals for managing problems.

Visualizing skills

If asked to think of someone you love, you are likely to get a visual image. People think in pictures as well as words, and some people do so more than others. Clients can use visual images to support or oppress themselves. For example, prior to job interviews, if clients visualize all the things that might go wrong, they make themselves anxious. Shy clients tend to visualize themselves behaving incompetently in social situations; angry clients often unrealistically visualize others' negative characteristics, and require more balanced pictures, and tense clients may visualize arousing rather than calming scenes. Frequently, clients fail to rehearse visually how they might use good rather than poor skills in situations.

Realistic decision-making

Clients may possess decision-making styles that lessen their effectiveness, for example, avoiding decisions or being too ready to fit in with others' decisions. Some clients are indecisive through being hypervigilant, worrying over every last detail; other clients are impulsive and consider relevant information insufficiently. In relationships, clients may be too competitive and not collaborate enough when making decisions. Some clients need to make major decisions more systematically, for instance, by generating and evaluating options. Other decision-making weaknesses include insufficient commitment to implementing decisions and poor planning.

HOW TO ASSESS

Helpers need to collaborate closely with clients not only to assess clients' thinking skills, but to develop clients' skills of doing this for themselves. Throughout this process, it is important that helpers offer supportive helping relationships. If helpers are rewarding listeners, clients are more inclined to disclose threatening material, acknowledge problems and look for the thinking-skills weaknesses that contribute to them. Since the purpose of assessing thinking is to redefine problems in skills terms, throughout this process helpers need to think in such terms themselves. However, when assessing thinking, you may choose not to use skills language openly, but leave this to your redefining statement. Following are additional helper skills for eliciting and assessing thinking.

Build a knowledge base

It is essential that helpers wishing to work with clients' thinking skills develop their knowledge about how people think, since you cannot assess what you do not know. In addition, you can increase your effectiveness if you are able to focus on a broad rather than on a narrow range of thinking skills. How can you develop your knowledge base? First, you can read the works of therapists who work with clients' thinking, sych as Beck, Ellis, Frankl, Lazarus, Meichenbaum and Yalom. In the bibliography I provide selected references. Second, you may read secondary sources such as my *Practical Counselling and Helping Skills* (third edition) and *Effective Thinking Skills*. Third, you can work on your own thinking skills either independently, or as clients, or in training groups. Some may wish to use my *Training Manual for Counselling and Helping Skills*, which has exercises in which readers work with their own thinking skills prior to focusing on those of others. Fourth, you may work with clients, preferably under supervision.

Introduce the PTC and STC frameworks

By using the PTC and STC frameworks, you can assist clients to be clearer that how they think affects how they feel and act. Ellis developed a simple ABC framework for thinking about thinking: A represents the activating event, B a person's rational or irrational beliefs about the activating event, and C the emotional and behavioural consequences of both A and B. Ellis maintains that much of the time people are only aware of what happens at points A and C.

The PTC and STC frameworks extend Ellis' ABC framework by distinguishing between problems and specific problematic situations and by incorporating skills language. The PTC framework applies to overall problems:

P your overall problem;
T your thoughts and thinking skills relating to the overall problem;
C your feelings and actions that are the consequences of P and T.

The STC framework applies to specific situations within overall problems:

S the situation;
T your thoughts and thinking skills relating to the situation;
C your feelings and actions that are the consequences of S and T.

An example of an overall problem and a specific situation within an overall problem is that of Ross. His overall problem is difficulty in communicating with his 6-year-old son Shane, a specific problematic situation is where Shane wants Ross to play football when he is reading the paper.

Collect information

Ways of eliciting and collecting information about clients' thinking include the following:

- *Client self-report.* Clients have various degrees of insight into their own thought process. Most often clients do not think of how they think in skills terms, and so are more likely to provide information on *what* they think rather than on *how* they think. However, once clients know what to look for, they may provide information on how they think too.

- *Thinking aloud.* You can encourage clients to 'think aloud' their thought processes before, during and after specific situations. You can say, 'Think back over the situation, and take me through in slow motion what your thoughts were before, during and after it.' An alternative instruction is, 'Close your eyes, visualize the situation, and take me through it in slow motion.'

- *Thought listing.* Clients can be asked to list and possibly rank-order thoughts relating to both problems and specific problematic situations.

- *Thought charting.* Thought charting entails clients filling in monitoring logs of how they thought in relation to specific situations. At its simplest, thought charting involves listing situations in one column and related thoughts and feelings in another column. It can also use a three-column STC format: situations in one column, thoughts in the next, and feelings and action consequences in the final column.

- *Counting.* Clients can count and record the frequency with which they have specific types of thoughts, for instance, catastrophic predictions. Counting can help clients to become aware of the repetitive nature of their thinking.

- *Questionnaires.* Clients can fill out questionnaires focused on thinking-skills weaknesses, such as unrealistic rules, anxious self-talk and attributional errors.

Use focusing-on-thinking questions

You can ask clients questions about both what they think and how they think. Also, after an initial, 'What did you think?', question, you can ask follow-up questions that encourage clients to be more specific, for example, 'When you thought they were trying to ridicule you, what made you think that?'. An alternative follow-up question might be, 'Where is the evidence?'. Partly by questions and partly by sensitive rewarding listening, you can encourage clients to look below the surface of initial thoughts to identify underlying thoughts. For example, 'Beyond their trying to ridicule you, were there any other thoughts you had?'. Here clients might respond with thoughts about previous similar situations in which they fared badly. Especially as clients become more aware, you can ask them to assess characteristic thinking errors and their consequences in specific situations.

Listen for language clues

Often without their realizing it, clients' language will provide you with valuable insights into their underlying thinking-skills weaknesses. For instance, comments like 'I had no choice', and use of verbs like 'I can't', rather than 'I won't', indicate clients who are inadequately owning responsibility for choices. Use of words like 'should', 'ought' and 'must' can indicate unrealistically rigid personal rules. Use of expressions like 'It's all their fault' and 'What are you going to do about my problem?' indicates failure to attribute cause accurately. Use of terms like 'She always' or 'He never' indicates inaccurately perceiving another and possibly oneself as well. Helpers need to check sensitively the hypotheses they form from clients' use of language – for instance, sometimes the reality may be 'He never'.

Backtrack from self-defeating feelings and actions

One way to assess thinking is to start with unwanted feelings and actions and then try to identify the thinking contributing to them. For instance, Kerry is conscious that she is extremely uptight about her upcoming performance review by her supervisor, Roberta, and that recently she has been tongue-tied in her presence. Using the STC framework, you could work with Kerry to elicit her thoughts and thinking-skills weaknesses, generating her unwanted feelings and actions. Sometimes, unwanted feelings – for instance guilt, shame, shyness, loneliness or resentment – provide both clues and motivation to explore thinking. Sometimes unwanted actions, such as domestic violence, stimulate exploring thinking. However, most often clients see that, like Kerry, they suffer from both self-defeating feelings and actions, and they become useful accomplices in discovering why.

Use role play and task assignment

You can conduct role plays with clients – for instance, saying no to an unreasonable request – and then explore their thoughts and feelings about this. Also, you can work with clients to identify tasks that they might perform outside helping – for instance, going to a senior citizens' club for the first time – and ask them to record how they thought and felt. Encourage clients to view such tasks as personal experiments designed to expand horizons and collect evidence.

Use a whiteboard

Whiteboards can enhance both assessment and learning. Their uses in assessing thinking include eliciting thoughts, storing them, refining them, showing linkages between them, and showing linkages within the PTC and STC frameworks. Helpers who use whiteboards clumsily – for instance, by being too school-teacherish – hamper clients' work. However, if you sensitively integrate the use of the whiteboard into your interviewing, you will probably find many clients prefer to work visually as well as verbally. Furthermore, whiteboards provide a means by which clients can actively contribute to the helping process: they can observe their contributions being recorded and see that they are valued.

Figure 7.1 *An interview room set up with a whiteboard*

FORM THINKING-SKILLS HYPOTHESES

When identifying and clarifying problems during stage 1 of the lifeskills model, helpers start forming hypotheses about how clients sustain problems with thinking-skills weaknesses. This process continues in stage 2, where helpers may gather more information to confirm or negate hypotheses. As you work with clients' thinking skills, you are likely to build up a fund of knowledge about which thinking-skills weaknesses may occur with different kinds of problems. For instance, many shy people have unrealistic rules about needing others' approval and use negative self-talk before, during and after social situations. People in marital conflicts may misperceive both themselves and their partners and also be prone to externalize the cause of their distress on to their partners. However, even though your previous experience may give you a start in knowing where to look, for each client you need check your hypotheses against the available facts.

Case example: Tony Fisher

Below is a brief excerpt from a case description of a careers counselling client called Tony Fisher:

Tony Fisher, aged 47, is married with two children. Tony had worked for a leading bank which he joined when he left secondary school 30 years ago. Starting as a clerk, he made his way up to management positions and finally became a well-paid systems analyst in the bank's electronic data-processing section. Tony planned to stay with the bank until he retired. Early last year Tony severed his ties with the bank after being told his job would no longer exist. The bank offered him a much less senior position as a relieving manager, albeit at the same salary. Tony turned down the offer, seeing it as too big a step backwards. Although the bank termed his departure 'early separation', Tony calls it being made redundant. Tony admits he had not seen it coming the way it did. He says that although he was unhappy with the way the bank squeezed him out, at least he was given the chance to make a respectable departure by being able to choose when he left. This episode badly knocked Tony's confidence and, despite looking for work, he has now been unemployed for nearly a year.

Following are some hypotheses suggesting a few thinking-skills weaknesses Tony may have exhibited in the above excerpt:

- *Not owning responsibility for choosing.* Tony did not realize the full extent of his choices. For instance, he could have stayed on while looking for other work either inside or outside the bank.
- *Choosing realistic personal rules.* Tony may have possessed unrealistic rules, such as, 'My career must always go forwards', and 'The bank must always appreciate me.' Both of these rules could weaken his flexibility in face of the bank's need to 'down-size.'
- *Choosing to perceive accurately.* Tony perceived that the bank squeezed him out. The evidence suggests that they offered him another job at the same salary, which is scarcely the same as being squeezed out. A possible alternative perception is that the bank appreciated his efforts and were trying to look after him during a harsh economic down-turn.
- *Attributing cause accurately.* Though Tony attributes the cause of his job loss to the bank, the evidence suggests that he brought his period of unemployment on himself.
- *Predicting accurately.* Tony may have had unrealistic predictions about the difficulty of obtaining work in a recessed economy. Also, if he had predicted the bank's difficulties earlier, he might have considered his job options sooner and even initiated a move.

The above case example tries to demonstrate the importance of not colluding in clients' versions of reality. Instead, lifeskills helpers look below the surface of what clients say to identify areas of faulty thinking. If Tony had seen a careers counsellor before choosing to leave the bank, and the counsellor had identified and worked on some of his potential thinking skills weaknesses, Tony's life might be much happier now.

ACTIVITIES

1. For each of the following thinking skills, assess your own strengths
   and weaknesses:
   > owning responsibility for choosing;
   > using coping self-talk;
   > choosing realistic personal rules;
   > choosing to perceive accurately;
   > attributing cause accurately;
   > predicting realistically;
   > setting realistic goals;
   > visualizing skills;
   > realistic decision-making.
2. Make a plan for developing your knowledge base about thinking
   skills.
3. Give reactions to each of the following strategies for assessing
   clients' thinking skills in initial sessions:
   > client self-report;
   > think aloud;
   > thought listing;
   > thought charting;
   > counting;
   > questionnaires;
   > focusing-on-thinking questions;
   > listening for language clues;
   > backtracking from self-defeating feelings and actions;
   > role play;
   > task assignment;
   > using a whiteboard.
4. Conduct an interview with a partner who discusses a specific
   problematic situation. Use some of the strategies assessing
   thinking skills listed in activity 3 to form hypotheses about one or
   two possible thinking-skills weaknesss. Afterwards, discuss your
   hypotheses and reverse roles.

EIGHT

How to assess action skills

The great end of life is not Knowledge but Action
T. H. Huxley

Action skills are observable behaviours. Using the inner–outer-game analogy, thinking skills represent clients' inner games and action skills represent their outer games. Helpers need always to assess action skills, since almost invariably clients' problems are sustained by action-skills weaknesses as well as by thinking-skills weaknesses.

WHAT TO ASSESS

When you assess action skills, you seek to answer questions like, 'What is the client doing or omitting to do?', 'How is the client doing it?', and 'What are the consequences for clients and others of how they act?'. Action skills tend to vary across situations. For example, action skills differ for parenting, managing stress, supervising colleagues, studying for exams, making friends and developing intimate relationships. When assessing action skills identify what relevant skills for clients' particular problems and their strengths and weakness in them are.

Many beginning helpers fail to assess action skills adequately because they focus too much on verbal skills. Clients' action skills can be divided into five main ways to send messages:

1. *Verbal messages.* Verbal messages are expressed in words. They are what clients say, partially say or omit to say.

2. *Voice messages.* Voice messages frame verbal messages. Dimensions of voice messages include volume, articulation, pitch, emphasis and rate.
3. *Body messages.* Body messages also frame verbal messages. Dimensions of body messages include gaze and eye contact, facial expression, posture, gestures, and clothing and grooming.
4. *Touch messages.* Touch messages are a special kind of body message involving physical contact with another. It is particularly important to assess use of touch in intimate relationships.
5. *Action messages.* The old maxim says, 'Actions speak louder than words.' Action messages are what clients actually do or fail to do as contrasted with what they say or how they say it.

When working with clients to assess action-skills strengths and weaknesses, be mindful of the following interrelated considerations.

- *Clarity.* How clearly do clients communicate? Do their messages come over loud and clear or, for various reasons, do they allow 'static' into their communication?
- *Consistency.* How consistent are clients' messages? Do their words match their actions? Does what they say match how they say it? Over a period of time, do they send the same or different messages? Inconsistencies not only make it harder for receivers to pick up messages, they also contribute to perceptions of senders as insincere.
- *Consequences.* What are the consequences for themselves and for others of how clients act? To what extent are the consequences harmful or helpful? How good are clients at perceiving and predicting the consequences of their actions?
- *Contexts.* Always assess clients' action-skills strengths and weaknesses within their relevant contexts. All behaviour is influenced by a network of implicit and explicit rules and expectations. Actions, such as kissing, that are appropriate in one context may be highly inappropriate in another. Sources of contextual rules and expectations include culture, race, social class, biological sex, sexual orientation, age, status and religion.
- *Omissions and avoidances.* What are clients not saying or doing that they might be saying and doing? What actions provide clues that they are avoiding dealing with situations directly? For example, Judy wishes to end her relationship with Sid. Instead of coming

right out with this, she indicates that she needs to spend more time at work, keeps increasing areas of her life that are off-limits to him, and becomes unreliable at keeping appointments.

HOW TO ASSESS

Helpers need to develop clients' skills at assessing their action skills. Within the context of supportive relationships, encourage clients to assess themselves rather than doing it all for them. Because they are more likely to think about how they act already, it should be easier for clients to assess their action skills than their thinking skills. Following are additional skills for assessing and encouraging self-assessment of action skills.

Build a knowledge base

Since action skills can differ so much across lifeskills areas, you need to build a broad knowledge base to know what to look for. In addition, you will need to develop more detailed knowledge about any kinds of problems or clienteles in which you specialize. For example, helpers specializing in assisting clients with sexual problems require knowledge of the different sexual dysfunctions and the effectiveness of different approaches to developing skills for managing them. Helpers working with substance abusers require specialized knowledge about working with people trying to curb their intake of specific types of drugs. Helpers working with post-operative cardiac patients require knowledge of the health risks of various kinds of activities and how best to assist clients to develop and maintain healthy habits.

Use the PTC and STC frameworks

By using the PTC and STC frameworks (see Chapter 7), you can assist clients to see the interrelationships between their feelings, thoughts and actions. For example, Neung has a problem getting his flat-mate Tuan to share the household chores. You can use the PTC (problem–thoughts–consequences) framework to get Neung disclosing and assessing how he thinks and acts in relation to the overall problem of increasing Tuan's domestic participation. In addition, examine one or more specific situations within the STC (situation–thought-consequences) framework to get more detailed information on how Neung actually behaves when confronted with Tuan's behaviour.

Collect information in interviews

Inside and outside interviews, helpers can collect information about how clients act. Following are some ways to collect information in interviews:

- *Listening to clients.* Invariably clients say how they act outside helping. While useful, client self-report has limitations, for example, clients tend to focus on verbal more than on voice and body messages, you never actually observe what happens, and they may edit what they say to protect themselves. What clients omit may be as important as what they report.
- *Observing clients.* Helpers are participant observers in the interview process. You can learn much from closely observing clients' verbal, voice and body messages. Sometimes clients' problems may take place before your very eyes, especially if they possess relating-skills weaknesses, for instance, difficulty in listening, disclosing, keeping eye contact and speaking audibly.
- *Focusing on action questions.* Focusing on action questions aims to elicit the specific details of how clients and others behaved, for instance, 'How did you behave?', and, 'How did he or she react?' You can cue clients to focus on voice and body as well as on verbal messages. Other dimensions of action skills include:
  - frequency, for instance, 'How often?' or 'How many times a day?';
  - duration, for instance, 'How long did it take you to? and 'Over what period?';
  - onset, for instance, 'When did you start behaving that way?'
- *Role play.* Clients can show you how they acted in specific situations. You can tell them that just hearing about how they acted does not give you a clear enough picture of what actually happened and that it might help both of you if they could show you. Cue clients to focus on voice and body as well as on verbal messages. If appropriate, act the role of the other person – for instance, the boss – in role plays.

- *Video-recording and play-back.* Observing video-recordings gives clients opportunities to see how they actually come across. You can use video feedback in individual work, for instance, with shy clients. Also, in marital work you can play back videos of partners who have been asked to show how they handle disputes, then ask them to identify their own and each other's helpful and harmful behaviours.

Collect information in real-life settings

Collecting information in interviews may not give you the opportunity to assess clients' action skills in specific problematic situations. Consequently, you may wish to collect information in clients' 'home' settings:

- *Helpers as observers.* Examples of helpers acting as observers outside interview sessions include observing a 'problem' child in class, on the playground or at home, an unassertive client asking for a drink in a bar, and a speech-anxious client giving a presentation.
- *Clients as observers.* Always encourage clients to become more aware of how they act in problem areas. You can set clients tasks, for instance, saying 'Hello' to classmates, and ask them to record how they got on. In addition, you can ask them to keep monitoring logs of how they acted in problematic situations. Figure 8.1 shows a possible format for such a log.
- *Third parties as observers.* With clients' permissions, you may ask third parties – for instance, teachers, spouses or supervisors – to collect information. Make sure third parties are clear about what to look for and how to record observations systematically.

Situation	How I acted		
	Verbal messages	Voice messages	Body messages

Figure 8.1 *A self-monitoring log*

FORM ACTION SKILLS HYPOTHESES

In stage 1 of the lifeskills helping model, when collecting descriptive information, you attempted to identify clients' main problem areas, and started making hypotheses not only about thinking-skills weaknesses but about action-skills weaknesses. Remember, the notion of clients possessing action-skills weaknesses does not preclude them from possessing strengths in the same areas. In stage 2 you may discard or refine stage 1 hypotheses and form and collect information about new hypotheses. Towards the end of stage 2, you should at the very least be in a position to share your action-skills hypotheses for either the client's main overall problem or a specific problematic situation. At this stage you form and check your main hypotheses, rather than state weaknesses in detail.

Case example: Tony Fisher

Tony Fisher is the career counselling client whose thinking-skills weaknesses were discussed in the previous chapter. Tony has now been unemployed for nearly a year. As a result of reviewing Tony's action skills for getting another job, his counsellor hypothesizes he possess weaknesses in the following skills areas:

making a resumé;
seeking information about advertised job opportunities;
creating and using an informal job contact network to
    find out about unadvertised opportunities;
creating and implementing a job marketing plan;
interview skills.

Tony's counsellor notes that in some of these areas – for instance, interview skills – the skills weaknesses include sending poor voice and body as well as poor verbal messages.

ACTIVITIES

1. Choose an action-skills area in your life, for instance, public speaking or saying no to a specific unreasonable request. In your chosen area or situation, assess your strengths and weaknesses at sending messages in each of the following ways: verbal, voice, body, touch, and by your actions.
2. Make a plan to develop your knowledge base about action skills specific to particular problems or clienteles with whom you work or may work in future.
3. Give your reactions to each of the following strategies for assessing clients' action skills:
   listening;
   observing;
   focusing on action questions;
   role play;
   video-recording and play-back;
   collecting information in real-life settings, with helpers as observers, clients as observers, and third parties as observers.
4. Conduct an interview with a partner who discusses a specific problematic situation. Use some of the strategies for assessing action skills listed in activity 3 to form hypotheses about one or two possible action-skills weaknesses. Afterwards, discuss your hypotheses and reverse roles.

NINE

How to redefine problems in skills terms

Every definition is dangerous.
Erasmus

In stage 2 of the lifeskills helping model, helpers move from describing clients' problems in everyday terms to redefining at least the clients' dominant or most pressing problem in skills terms. 'Teeing up problems' is a colloquial expression for redefining problems. Good redefinitions break clients' problems down and identify the main thinking-skills and action-skills weaknesses sustaining them. You set up problems so that clients can work on them. In subsequent sessions, problems may be still further broken down into their component skills. Also, in later sessions, new problems may emerge that require clarifying, assessing and redefining.

Most clients are in states of 'stuckness' rather than 'sickness'. Based on previously collected material, skills redefinitions provide clients with 'handles' or 'keys' with which to work for change. Skills redefinitions are sets of hypotheses about skills weaknesses sustaining problems. As hypotheses, they are subject to continuous testing and also to minor or major reformulations as helping progresses. No moral judgement is attached to the term 'skills weaknesses': rather, these are problematic skills on which clients need work to manage problems better both now and in future.

Both overall problems and specific problematic situations within overall problems can be redefined in skills terms. For instance, James comes to see a helper highly anxious about a driving test he is taking in a week. In such a case, the helper would initially work with James' immediate situation rather than with his overall problem of assessment anxiety.

GUIDELINES FOR SKILLS REDEFINITIONS

Redefinitions of clients' problems into skills terms are for clients' even more than for helpers' benefits. Below are some guidelines for good skills redefinitions of clients' problems:

- *Use the T format.* For each problem or problematic situation, you can use the two-column T format, with the columns titled 'Thinking-skills weaknesses' and 'Action-skills weaknesses'. I prefer having thinking skills in the left-hand column, since clients' inner-game skills tend to precede their outer-game skills.
- *Use skills language.* Some beginning helpers learning the lifeskills model fail to use skills language when redefining problems. Do not make this mistake. Skills language helps clients to work on specific weaknesses both during and after helping.
- *State skills weaknesses as hypotheses.* You could even use the word 'hypotheses' in your T-format column headings, for instance, 'Thinking-skills hypotheses' and 'Action-skills hypotheses'. Clients should clearly understand that skills-weakness hypotheses are open to confirmation or modification in the light of emerging information.
- *Show clear links to information provided by clients.* Always do the spadework before suggesting skills redefinitions. Clients are more likely to understand and accept skills redefinitions if they see a clear relationship between the information they have provided and the thinking- and action-skills weaknesses you suggest.
- *Focus on high-priority problems.* In initial sessions, skills redefinitions should take into account clients' needs to make progress in at least one major problem area or situation. It is better to do one skills redefinition well than more superficially.
- *Do not overload clients with detail.* Too much detail confuses clients, so present only important skills weaknesses. Identifying one or two central thinking- and action-skills weaknesses may suffice. It is important that you correctly identify the skills weaknesses and that clients clearly understand them.

- *Be specific about skills weaknesses.* Avoid vagueness – for instance, do not write, 'poor assertion skills', without identifying the specific assertion skills that are poor; write instead, 'poor skills at requesting behaviour changes', or, 'poor skills at saying no to unreasonable requests.' You could even go further and 'flag' the main verbal, voice, and body messages in which the client is weak, such as absence of 'I' statements, soft voice and poor eye contact.
- *State skills weaknesses that are easily translatable into working goals.* The whole purpose of identifying skills weaknesses is that they lead to stating working goals. For instance, 'poor skills at saying no to unreasonable requests' is easily translatable into 'develop good skills at saying no to unreasonable requests'.

FURTHER SKILLS FOR REDEFINING PROBLEMS

Below are some further helper skills for how to redefine clients' problems in skills terms.

Make a transition statement

In earlier structuring statements, you are likely to have asked clients to describe problems more fully so that together you can identify possible skills that they need to work on. Later, you can make a statement that provides a transition from assessing problems to redefining them in skills terms. In this transition statement you may further explain reasons for redefining problems in skills terms. Below is an example of a transition statement:

Well, Ben, for the previous half hour or so we've been exploring in some detail your problems in getting on with your father, whom you perceive as very difficult. Despite this, you say you would like to improve your relationship with him. As we've been talking, I've been making mental notes about a number of ways that you seem to be thinking and acting that might be interfering with your attaining your goal. Without implying any criticism, I'm going to state these tentatively on the whiteboard as 'thinking-skills weaknesses' and 'action-skills weaknesses'. The idea is that once we agree on where your weaknesses may lie, we can then translate these into goals for developing strengths. I will check my suggestions with you to see if we can arrive at a common view concerning skills on which you need to work.

Work together with clients

A risk in putting skills redefinitions on the whiteboard is that you become too didactic, so aim to create an emotional climate where clients feel safe to make suggestions, ask for clarification, and even reject some of your ideas. Given good rationales, most clients will appreciate your efforts to redefine problems. However, some may view this as too mechanistic. In such instances, try to discuss and work through their reservations. Other clients may rightly view as premature a redefinition of their problems in skills terms, for instance, if sharing grief. Still other clients may be unready to acknowledge their role in sustaining their difficulties and require more time to lower their defences.

You need to work closely with clients to increase the accuracy and acceptability of your skills redefinitions. Take seriously their suggestions and requests for clarification, and check whether they agree with your suggestions, rather than assume that they do so. If clients have reservations, explore these further and make any appropriate modifications to your redefinitions.

You can increase the acceptability of skills redefinitions if you incorporate words and expressions that have meaning for clients. For instance, Amanda was a client whose negative self-talk contributed to her anger. The word 'pride' resonated with her; consequently, one of her thinking skills weaknesses was listed as 'negative self-talk, e.g. letting my pride get in the way'.

Attend to feelings

When redefining problems in skills terms, you need to attend to clients' feelings. Clients can have positive and negative feelings about both the processes and outcomes of redefining their problems. Also, certain clients experience difficulty in acknowledging responsibility for having problems and for possessing specific skills weaknesses that sustain these problems. You require tact and patience to offer explanations, deal with reservations and lessen defensiveness. On the positive side, good redefinitions of problems in skills terms can encourage and motivate clients. Whereas previously they were stuck, now they may see glimmers of hope from knowing where to work.

Encourage between-session learning

From the start, encourage clients to take an active part in helping. Also, use the time between sessions to good effect. For instance, clients can learn much from listening to cassettes of helping sessions, which may not only consolidate their understanding of your redefinitions, but also give them further opportunity to suggest alterations or amendments, and assist them in remembering redefinitions. Another aid to remembering redefinitions is for clients to write them down. Clients can keep helping records or files. Items from stages 1 and 2 of the lifeskills helping model for storage in such files include self-monitoring logs and redefinitions in skills terms.

EXAMPLES OF REDEFINITIONS IN SKILLS TERMS

Example 1: Tony Fisher

Tony Fisher is the unemployed, 47-year-old, former bank executive mentioned in Chapters 7 and 8. Figure 9.1 shows a T-format redefinition in skills terms of Tony's problem in getting another job.

Example 2: Ben Street

Ben Street, aged 18, comes to counselling worried about his deteriorating relationship with his father. Ben is disturbed about the aggressive way his father sometimes relates to his mother, and he handles his difficulties with his father by alternating aggression with withdrawal. Ben admits his father does a lot for him and might respond favourably to moves to improve the relationship. Figure 9.2 shows a T-format redefinition in skills terms of Ben's problem in his relationship with his father.

Thinking-skills weaknesses	Action-skills weaknesses
Insufficiently owning responsibility for choices in life	Making a resumé
Unsystematic career decision-making skills	Seeking information about advertised job opportunities
Unrealistic personal rules, for example, about achievement	Creating and using an informal job contact network
Perceiving self inaccurately, for example, job skills	Creating and implementing a job marketing plan
Negative self-talk surrounding job interviews	Poor interview skills (verbal, voice and body messages)

Figure 9.1 *Tony Fisher's T-format redefinition*

Thinking-skills weaknesses	Action-skills weaknesses
Possessing unclear goals for relationship with Dad	Listening skills
Unrealistic personal rules, for example, demanding approval	Self-disclosing skills
	Showing-appreciation skills
Inaccurately attributing cause, for example, Dad should make first move, assuming too much responsibility for Dad and Mum's relationship	General conversational skills
	Sharing-pleasant-activities skills
Perceiving self and Dad inaccurately	
Negative self-talk, surrounding talking with Dad	

Figure 9.2 *Ben Street's T-format redefinition*

Example 3: Nancy Coogan

Nancy Coogan, aged 46, returned to the workforce as a secretary in a college chemistry department. After a few months Nancy was appointed office manager, a job she now experiences considerable trouble holding down. Figure 9.3 shows a T-format redefinition in skills terms of Nancy's problem in managing the office.

Thinking-skills weaknesses	Action-skills weaknesses
Insufficiently owning responsibility for being a chooser at work	Giving instructions assertively (poor verbal, voice and body messages)
Unrealistic personal rules, for example, everyone must approve of me, I must be the perfect manager	Getting-support skills, for example, from department head
Inaccurately perceiving, for example, focusing on own negatives, discounting positive feedback	
Negative self-talk, for example, about confronting difficult colleagues	

Figure 9.3   *Nancy Coogan's T-format redefinition*

ACTIVITIES

1. Think of one or more common problems of a client population with whom you either currently work or would like to work. Make a T-format worksheet for each problem and redefine it by identifying some central thinking-skills weaknesses and action-skills weaknesses.

2. Work with a partner who acts as a client who comes to helping with a specific problem. Using skills from stages 1 and 2 of the lifeskills helping model, conduct an interview to the point where you redefine your client's problem in skills terms. If possible, use a whiteboard and record your interview. Afterwards, discuss your interview with your partner and reverse roles. Also, play back your recording as homework.

TEN

How to state working goals

What is the use of running when we are not on the right road?
German proverb

Stage 2 of the lifeskills model helping ends with one or more redefinitions in skills terms of clients' problems. In stage 3, helpers restate problems redefined in skills terms into working goals and plan how best to attain them (see Figure 10.1).

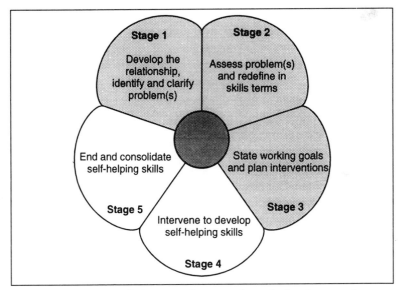

Figure 10.1   *Stage 3 State working goals and plan interventions*

PROBLEM MANAGEMENT AND PROBLEMATIC SKILLS GOALS

An issue in helping is how much to focus on managing immediate problems as against problematic skills sustaining problems. For instance, Tony Fisher, the 47-year old former bank executive, has a current problem about finding another job. Tony's goals could be stated in problem-management outcome terms, for instance, 'obtaining a position that uses my banking skills within a stipulated salary range'. Here both helper and Tony state a goal that is relevant only to his current problem. A problematic-skills approach to Tony's getting another job problem aims to identify thinking-skills strengths and action-skills strengths he requires, but insufficiently possesses, to attain his problem-management goal of getting another job. This approach can go still further, to state goals about developing Tony's skills for obtaining not only current employment but future employment. If career decision making is viewed as a single problem-management task, rather than a set of skills, helpers may play down or ignore some thinking skills that Tony requires beyond straightforward decision-making skills, for instance, possessing realistic personal rules about achievement. Also, they may fail to impart career decision-making skills so that Tony obtains self-helping skills that inoculate him against the negative effects of future job losses, including retirement.

One of lifeskills helping's major assumptions is that problems repeat themselves – what is termed the *repetition phenomenon*. Clients who get anxious about exams have probably had similar past problems and will probably have similar future problems. Life can go around in negative circles, so wherever possible, helpers should try to break into these negative circles by assisting clients in attending to the underlying problematic skills that sustain their vulnerability to future similar problems. During the intervention stage, problematic skills goals may be broken down still further so that clients are clear as to the sequences of choices entailed in targeted skills.

ADVANTAGES AND RISKS OF WORKING GOALS

Stating working goals has both advantages and risks. Following are some advantages. Establishing problem-management and problematic skills goals with clients assists them in assuming personal responsibility for their lives, so that they create their own directions rather than following others' paths as if they were their own. Good statements of working goals provide bases for planning interventions and assessing helping outcomes. They give clients focus, assist their motivation and increase their persistence. In addition, good statements of working goals heighten the likelihood of clients retaining targeted skills as self-helping skills afterwards. Clients are more likely to remember and strive for clearly stated targeted skills strengths than if no such statements exist.

There are risks to stating working goals. However, most risks are not inherent in stating goals: rather, they stem from stating them the wrong way or prematurely. If redefinitions of clients' problems in skills terms are inaccurate or superficial, so may be any statements of working goals emanating from these redefinitions. Another risk is that working goals represent helpers' rather than clients' agendas. Intentionally or unintentionally, helpers may fail to check clients' reactions and negotiate working goals. Working goals that represent helpers' rather than clients' agendas may elicit resistances; clients may say 'yes' to such goals, but behave 'no' and lack commitment to implementing them. Furthermore, even if agreed upon, over-ambitious working goals place unrealistic expectations on both parties.

Another risk is that working goals restrict focus. They may be too narrowly stated in the first place. Also, helpers may focus on initial working goals at the expense of paying adequate attention to emerging working goals. Still another risk is that when stating working goals, helpers attend insufficiently to clients' feelings – for instance, some clients require more support and space before they are ready to work directly on their contributions to problems.

HELPER THINKING SKILLS

How helpers think influences how they set goals. Following are some thinking skills to bear in mind when setting and stating goals:

Use lifeskills language

When you state overall goals you are more likely to use everyday language. For instance, Tony Fisher wants to get another job, Ben

Street to have a better relationship with his father, and Nancy Coogan to become a more effective office manager (see Chapter 9). Overall goals provide visions of what clients want; working goals provide signposts of how to get there. Whereas overall goals reflect ends, working goals reflect means. With the lifeskills helping model, working goals should always be stated in skills terms. For instance, at the end of this chapter I give statements of Tony's, Ben's and Nancy's working goals. These working goals are the reverse or 'flip-side; of redefinitions of problems in skills terms. Whereas redefinitions focus on identifying skills weaknesses, statements of working goals focus on turning skills weaknesses into skills strengths. The emphasis shifts from overcoming negatives to attaining positives.

Attribute accurately

'Who is responsible for setting goals?' Beware of attributing too much responsibility for forming working goals to yourself. If you assume too much control over the goal-setting process, you risk your efforts being resisted during helping and neglected afterwards. Working goals need to be owned by helpers and clients in different ways. Helpers need to own working goals as being consistent with their ways of working and as guides for how to help clients, whereas clients need to own them as guides for how to help themselves. Helpers should own goals in 'professional' ways, whereas clients should own them in 'personal' ways.

Clients' commitment to attaining working goals is crucial. Clients are more likely to show commitment if they have contributed to shaping the goals. Working goals need to be realistic, perceived by clients as relevant, consistent with their values and comprehensible. Furthermore, helpers and clients should consider stating time frames for both initially attaining and then maintaining working goals.

Possess realistic personal and helping rules

Goal setting is one of the main areas in which helpers' own inner-game 'stuff' can interfere with their effectiveness. Below are some unrealistic personal rules that could negatively influence how you state working goals:

- 'I must get quick results.'
- 'I must always be the one who knows what's best.'

- 'Working goals must always be set very high.'
- 'I must never make mistakes when initially setting working goals.'
- 'My clients must always agree with everything I suggest.'
- 'I must never modify or revise working goals.'

All the above unrealistic rules can place unnecessary demands on yourself and your clients. If any of them 'ring a bell' for you, dispute them and try to replace them with more rational rules. Ideally, you form and state working goals in clients' best interests and not on the basis of your own lack of personal development.

Perceive accurately

Perceiving clients accurately is always difficult, since all helpers tend to bring their own 'stuff' into helping. If, during stages 1 and 2 of the lifeskills helping model, you do not listen properly and so misperceive what your clients communicate, inevitably you risk introducing errors when you state working goals in stage 3. Also, if you do not attend to clients' feedback about working goals, you further risk their lack of both understanding and commitment. You are always at risk of denying and distorting what clients say.

Predict realistically

A statement of working goals is basically a prediction that if clients attain all or part of them, then they will make progress in managing their problems. You may have wrongly predicted clients' main skills weaknesses, and others may emerge as more important. Also, you may overpredict or underpredict clients' capacities to develop skills strengths. To counteract tendencies to inaccurate predictions when stating goals, you can review probability more stringently, including assessing clients' coping skills and support factors more thoroughly.

HELPER ACTION SKILLS

Helper action skills for stating working goals are similar to those for redefining problems in skills terms.

Make a transition statement

In your earlier structuring statements, you may have introduced the idea of translating skills redefinitions into statements of working goals. For instance, part of the example in Chapter 9 of the helper's transition statement to making a skills redefinition of Ben's problem in relating better with his father was, 'The idea is that once we agree on where your weaknesses may lie, we can then translate these into goals for developing strengths.'

Once you have made and discussed your redefinition, you may make a further transition statement along the following lines:

> Ben, we have now identified and agreed upon some possible thinking and action skills weaknesses through which you may contribute to your poor relationship with your father. Your overall goal is to improve your relationship with him. By reversing your possible skills weaknesses into positive objectives or working goals, you can get a clear idea of where you need to work to develop skills strengths. I'll do this by making some relatively simple word changes on the whiteboard and then ask for your reactions.

Use a whiteboard

A great advantage of using a whiteboard is the ease with which you can rub out the negative parts of your redefinitions in skills terms to turn them into positive statements of goals. You can also work together with clients to ensure the revised wording suits them. Once you and your clients are happy with the statements of working goals on the whiteboard, both of you need to take them down for your records. You and your clients still need to plan how to attain working goals and to monitor your progress in doing so.

Work together with clients

Using checking skills, attending to feelings and being flexible are three ways in which you can work together with clients to increase the accuracy and acceptance of goals statements. Always check clients' reactions to working goals. One reason for checking is that clients may require further clarification regarding some goals, in addition, clients

Figure 10.2 *The author using a whiteboard to state working goals*

may feel threatened by seeing working goals written up before them, because they fear both the processes and outcomes of change. Attend to their feelings of threat and work through them as well as possible. Your flexibility is important for many reasons, including using language that has meaning for clients, not overloading them with too many working goals, and getting the balance right between managing problems and working with underlying problematic skills.

EXAMPLES OF STATEMENTS OF WORKING GOALS

Following are redefinitions in skills terms for Tony Fisher, Ben Street and Nancy Coogan.

Case Example 1: Tony Fisher

Overall goal: To obtain suitable employment

Working goals

Thinking-skills goals	Action-skills goals
Develop my skills of:	Develop my skills of:
owning responsibility for choices;	making a resumé
systematic career decision making;	seeking information about advertised job opportunities;
possessing realistic personal rules, for example, about achievement;	creating and using an informal job contact network;
perceiving myself accurately, for example, job skills;	creating and implementing a job marketing plan;
coping self-talk, for example, for job interviews	interview skills (verbal, voice and body messages).

Figure 10.3 *Tony Fisher's redefinition in skills terms*

Case Example 2: Ben Street

Overall goal: To relate better with my father

Working goals

Thinking-skills goals	Action-skills goals
Develop my skills of:	Develop my listening skills
setting clear goals for my relationship with Dad;	Develop my self-disclosing skills
possessing realistic personal rules, for example, concerning approval;	Develop my showing-appreciation skills
accurately attributing cause, for example, I can make the first move:	Develop my general conversational skills
perceiving myself and Dad accurately;	Develop my sharing-pleasant activities skills
coping self-talk, for example, before and after talking with Dad	

Figure 10.4   *Ben Street's redefinition in skills terms*

Case Example 3: Nancy Coogan

Overall goal: Manage the office more effectively, including my feelings about it

Working goals

Thinking-skills goals	Action-skills goals
Develop my skills of:	Develop my skills of giving instructions assertively (verbal, voice and body messages)
owning responsibility for being a chooser at work:	
	Develop my getting-support skills, for example, from department head
possessing realistic personal rules, for example, I don't need everyone's approval, I don't have to be perfect;	
accurately perceiving, for example, acknowledging my strengths, acknowledging positive feedback;	
coping self-talk, for example, about confronting difficult colleagues	

Figure 10.5   *Nancy Coogan's redefinition in skills terms*

ACTIVITIES

1. For each of the following thinking-skills areas, assess whether and
   how your thinking-skills strengths and weaknesses might
   influence the way you state working goals:
       use lifeskills language;
       attribute accurately;
       possess realistic personal and helping rules;
       perceive accurately;
       predict realistically.
2. In the first activity of Chapter 9 you wrote out redefinitions in
   skills terms of common problems of a client population with
   whom you either currently work or would like to work. For each
   problem, make a further T-format worksheet and restate each
   thinking-skills weakness and action-skills weakness as working
   goals.

ELEVEN

How to plan interventions

It is a bad plan that admits of no modification.
Publilius Syrus

Statements of working goals form the basis for choosing interventions. Helpers and clients agree where they want to go, but then need to plan how to get there.

INTERVENTIONS AND PLANS

A distinction exists between interventions and plans. *Interventions* are intentional behaviours on the part of both helpers and clients, designed to attain specific thinking-skills or action-skills working goals. Alternative words for interventions are strategies, procedures or techniques. Interventions can be either helper-centred or client-centred. With helper-centred interventions, helpers do things to or for clients; with client-centred interventions, helpers encourage clients to build their own skills. For example, you can either relax clients or teach them how to relax themselves. Client-centred interventions that last beyond helping are strongly recommended.

Plans are statements that combine and sequence interventions. The term 'working plan' is preferable to 'treatment plan', since plans outline how clients can actively attain working goals rather than be passively treated by helpers. Plans are the maps or diagrams that enable helpers and clients to get from where they are to where they want to be.

CHOOSING INTERVENTIONS

Helpers as practitioner-researchers choose interventions on the basis of hypotheses about how clients are most likely to attain working goals. Following are some criteria for choosing interventions.

Acceptability to clients

Clients come to helping with their own goals. When they have time and motivation only for managing immediate problems, longer-term interventions focused on building underlying problematic skills are inappropriate. Even where clients have time and motivation to work on thinking- and action-skills weaknesses, they still need to understand, at least at a minimal level, and be comfortable with any interventions you suggest, as they are otherwise unlikely to work on interventions during and after helping.

Helper competence to administer interventions

Beginning helpers tend to possess limited repertoires of interventions, which restrict how they can work. Sometimes such helpers jump in too quickly with interventions they do not understand. However, on other occasions, they may hold back unnecessarily through lack of confidence. Beginning helpers are advised to focus on building a range of central helping interventions. For instance, in the area of thinking skills, they might initially focus on core skills, such as assisting clients in identifying, disputing and reformulating unrealistic personal rules, in identifying inaccurate perceptions, generating alternatives and choosing the 'best-fit' perception, and in identifying negative self-talk and developing coping self-talk skills for handling specific situations. In the area of action skills, assisting clients in acquiring the verbal, voice and body skills of making assertive requests for others to change their behaviour has widespread relevance. Helpers can understand interventions, but still lack the training skills to deliver them properly, and even experienced helpers need to work on building their range of interventions and on how effectively they deliver them. Central helper training skills are discussed in the next chapter.

Theoretical and research support for interventions

All helpers operate within implicit and explicit theoretical frameworks that attempt to explain and predict behaviour. The theoretical framework underpinning this book is outlined in *Practical Counselling and Helping Skills: How to Use the Lifeskills Helping Model* (third edition). Try to keep abreast of the continuing education and research literature in areas in which you help or intend helping. You can read books and journals, attend workshops and courses, and arrange for individual and peer supervision. Develop a positive attitude to continuing development of your helping knowledge and skills.

Client considerations

Many client considerations influence choosing interventions. For instance, highly anxious clients may require interventions with a more nurturing and healing emphasis prior to more task-oriented and self-helping interventions. Consider clients' motivation to accept and implement interventions and the likelihood of their rejecting or resisting interventions. Appropriateness of interventions also varies according to age, maturity and ability to comprehend how to carry through interventions. Ultimately clients have to understand the choices involved so that they can implement lifeskills on their own. Where necessary, take into account clients' cultures when choosing and implementing interventions, for instance, the greater emphasis on individualism in Western cultures and on harmonious group relationships in Asian cultures. Also, consider the influence of sex-role conditioning and any need for clients to become more gender aware. A host of practical considerations may influence choice of interventions, for example, clients' upcoming tasks, their time and financial constraints, the presence or absence of people to support their change efforts outside helping, and your availability.

Appropriateness of group interventions

Would individual clients develop targeted skills strengths better if they joined lifeskills training groups instead of, concurrently or after individual helping? Some clients might benefit from joining longer-term interactional groups. Considerations relevant to selecting group interventions include availability of appropriate groups and clients' willingness to participate in them.

Appropriateness of referral

You may consider that clients should see someone else either in conjunction with seeing you or instead of you. For example, the client may have a specialized problem, such as a sexual dysfunction or a career decision, and you may know someone more expert than yourself to assist him or her. Sometimes, you can make referrals and still work with clients – for instance, when working with unemployed clients, you can refer them to attend workshops on interview skills.

KINDS OF PLANS

Almost invariably, helpers use interventions in combination rather than in isolation. Consequently, they need to develop plans or hypotheses about how best to use interventions in combination. Following are broad categories of plans:

Problem-management plans

Here the immediate problem rather than the underlying problematic skills is the focus. For instance, Wendy has an upcoming visit from her in-laws whom she thinks always criticize her. A problem-management plan looks at strategies Wendy can use right now to manage both her in-laws and her feelings towards them. Also, the plan suggests how, in the time available. Wendy can become proficient in the strategies, for instance, by means of role plays with her helper. Little attempt is made to develop systematically Wendy's skills for future interactions with her parents-in-law. Problem-management plans might be better named 'situation-management plans', since their focus is on coping with immediate situations rather than on managing on-going problems.

Problematic skills: structured plans

Plans may be of varying degrees of structure. Following are variations of structured plans:

- *Predetermined structured plans.* Here helpers and clients decide to structure helping around existing skills development packages or programmes, for instance, for developing skills such as relaxation, parenting or overcoming agoraphobia. These programmes are likely to have learning materials, such as a client's manual and accompanying audio-cassettes or videotapes.
- *Tailor-made structured plans.* Here helpers map out programmes for individual clients to help them to attain targeted skills. Tailor-made plans have the advantage of being geared to the specific needs and learning abilities of individual clients. Also, clients can become part of the planning process. Thus tailor-made structured plans are more suggested than prescribed.
- *Partly structured plans.* Helpers can develop plans that have elements of structure, yet fall short of being step-by-step structured programmes. For instance, a partly structured plan to assist Tony Fisher (see Chapter 10) to get another job might allow some open-ended counselling sessions, interpersed with structured activities such as group testing sessions and attending workshops on job-getting and interview skills. A partly structured plan for assisting Ben Street (see Chapter 10) to relate better to his father might entail spending the second session focusing on developing his thinking skills, the third session developing his action skills, and the fourth session consolidating both his thinking and action skills for the future.

Problematic skills: open plans

Open plans allow helpers without predetermined structure to choose which interventions to use to attain which working goals and when. Bearing in mind targeted skills, helpers and clients collaborate to set session agendas and work with material that clients bring into sessions. Open plans have the great advantage of flexibility. Clients may be more motivated to work on skills and material that have relevance at any given time instead of being restricted to predetermined agendas.

PLANNING CONSIDERATIONS

Following are some considerations when planning interventions:

- *When to plan?* You can make plans inside or outside of sessions. Open plans only involve within-session time, but more elaborate plans may entail your setting aside sufficient time outside of sessions to think them through thoroughly.
- *Whom to involve?* If you have negotiated your redefinition in skills terms and working goals with clients you will already have involved them. At the very least, since clients bear much of the responsibility for implementing plans, always check that they are comfortable with them. Often you can involve them in the planning process early on. Also, with adult clients' permission, you may choose to involve significant others in plans, for instance, partners. With children, keeping their best interests in mind, use your discretion about asking their permission to involve others.
- *What time frame?* Consider the time frame for your plan. For various client and helper reasons, you may have limited time. Also, consider whether you should plan booster sessions.
- *How to sequence content?* Sequence activities in plans systematically. For instance, when planning to impart the skill of choosing realistic personal rules, a logical sequence might entail saying what you mean by unrealistic rules, and then focusing on identifying, disputing, reformulating and maintaining self-supporting rules, in that order. Another consideration in sequencing content is to try to arrange that clients get early success experiences from using targeted skills, since such successes are likely to enhance motivation and persistence. Sequencing easier before more difficult tasks heightens clients' chances of succeeding.
- *How to train?* Consider what training skills you will use to attain each working goal and when. Training skills include verbal presentations, demonstrations, coaching and homework. Also consider what training materials you need, for instance, handouts, manuals and cassettes.
- *How to emphasize self-helping?* From the start, build in a focus on maintaining trained skills as self-helping skills for afterwards. Ensure that clients learn to instruct themselves in targeted skills. Emphasize homework assignments in real-life settings, and identify and develop strategies for dealing with high-risk situations where clients might experience difficulty in using targeted skills.

WORKING WITH CLIENTS

In earlier structuring statements, you may have signalled that once you agree on working goals you will discuss ways of attaining them. Once you have finished presenting and checking working goals and they have been written down, make a transition statement like this:

'Now we are clear as to what skills strengths you need to develop, let's discuss how best to go about this.'
'We've just agreed upon where we want to go, now let's plan how to get there.'

There are many ways to enhance clients' commitment to implementing plans. Getting them to participate in planning has many advantages, for instance, enhancing their understanding of goals, steps in the plan, and the reasons for them. Also, participation increases their sense of ownership and keeps plans relevant and realistic. Other ways to foster commitment include asking for feedback, identifying reservations and giving clear explanations and answers to queries.

All plans imply or state contractual obligations for both helpers and clients. You may need to clarify your expectations of each other – for example, you may state that you expect regular attendance over a specified number of sessions, completion of homework assignments, and regular process reviews. Once you and your clients have decided upon plans, you can start implementing them.

ACTIVITIES

1. Write out or discuss the importance of each of the following criteria for choosing interventions:
   acceptability to clients;
   helper competence to administer interventions;
   theoretical and research support;
   client considerations, such as anxiety level;
   appropriateness of group interventions;
   appropriateness of referral.
2. In the second activity of Chapter 10, you stated working goals for common problems of a client population with whom you either

currently work or would like to work. For each set of working goals, make out a plan for how you might assist a client to attain them. Take into account the following considerations:

When to plan?
Whom to involve?
What time frame?
How to sequence content?
How to train?
How to emphasize self-helping?

TWELVE

How to use training skills

He [she] who can, does. He [she] who cannot, teaches.
George Bernard Shaw

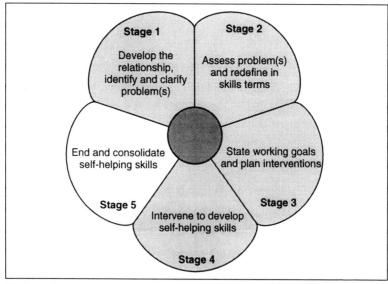

Figure 12.1   *Stage 4 Intervene to develop self-helping skills*

In stage 4 of the lifeskills helping model, helpers choose from a range of interventions to develop clients' self-helping skills (see Figure 12.1). Some central thinking skills are relevant to most interventions. Broadly defined, training skills include offering supportive helping relationships and assessing clients. Here, the focus is on the skills of how to deliver interventions. Below are some examples of helpers who use poor training skills:

> Bernadette is a marital counsellor working with a client, Louise. Bernadette launches into a long-winded and muddled explanation of the skill of perceiving your partner accurately by not jumping to conclusions that have little basis in fact. Since the skill was never clearly articulated, Louise does not learn it.

> For some time Terry has avoided confronting a work colleague whom he perceived as putting him down. Terry and his supervisor, Viki, discuss various strategies for doing this and agree on one of them. At no stage does Viki show Terry how to implement the strategy.

> Prue is a bedding salesperson terrified at the prospect of an upcoming presentation before 25 people. Her staff counsellor, Neil, talks about and demonstrates the skill of coping self-talk. However, he fails to get Prue to use the skill in front of him so that he can give her feedback. Had Neil done so, he would have found that Prue had still to develop specific coping statements that were right for her.

Helpers as trainers require good skills in the three broad areas of *tell*, *show* and *do*. In the above examples,. Bernadette failed to *tell* Louise clearly about the skill of perceiving accurately by not jumping to unwarranted conclusions: Viki failed to *show* Terry how to confront his difficult colleague; and Neil never gave Prue the opportunity to *do* coping self-talk in front of him and receive feedback. To put it another way, helpers require speaking skills, demonstrating skills and coaching skills. In addition, they require assigning-homework skills.

Always use training skills in the context of supportive helping relationships. Helpers should offer clients companionship in their learning journeys. The emotional climate in which clients work best is one in which they feel safe to take risks, reveal vulnerabilities, experience feelings, examine the consequences of their choices, and share difficulties in implementing skills.

SPEAKING SKILLS

Helpers require good speaking skills to present lifeskills information to clients. Some helpers are much better in the relatively passive role of making listening responses to clients rather than in the more active role of imparting information. Virtually all helpers need to work on their presenting-information skills.

Manage speech anxiety

Helping is never free from anxiety on the part of both helpers and clients. Your anxiety may become greater when you present skills information to clients. You may not understand the skill properly, and/or you may have poor delivery skills. Possessing knowledge of the subject matter and developing your delivery skills are two approaches to managing speech anxiety. In addition, you may think yourself into trouble, so a third approach is to work on your thinking skills to lessen the chances of helper MATO (my anxiety takes over).

You may contribute to speech anxiety by using negative self-talk, for instance, 'I'm going to make a mess of this presentation.' If so, counteract this by making coping self-talk statements like, 'Relax. Speak slowly and clearly.' You may expect too much of yourself, for instance, your unrealistic rules may include, 'I must never make mistakes', and, 'My clients must learn quickly.' If so, dispute the realism of your rules and replace them with more rational ones. You may inaccurately perceive your skills at presenting information, for instance, thinking you are better or worse than you are. In addition, you may be hypersensitive to cues of negative feedback from clients. If you become aware of perceiving inaccurately, appraise the evidence realistically and make inferences that fit the available facts best.

Prepare clear content

Helpers should present skills clearly enough so that clients can instruct themselves in them. Even though you may present lifeskills information to only one client at a time, you still need to know your material thoroughly. When presenting skills for the first time, prepare a systematic outline of the structure of the skill. For instance, the structure of a presentation on developing realistic personal rules to manage exam anxiety might cover the following areas: reason for skill, identifying anxiety-engendering rules, disputing unrealistic rules, reforming unrealistic into realistic rules, and changing actions along with rules. You should not present all of this at once. When training individual clients in skills, you can interact and go at a pace congenial to them.

How you use language is important. When introducing and describing targeted skills, use skills language. Also, adjust your language so you are easily comprehensible to clients – for instance, the term 'rewarding listening' may communicate more clearly to non-professionals than does 'empathic understanding'. Use practical examples that involve clients' own material and experiences, and be prepared to use humour to lighten and enhance learning.

Develop delivery skills

When you present material to clients, send good voice, body and audio-visual messages. You seek to hold clients' interest and avoid them getting a bad case of MEGO (my eyes glaze over). Perhaps even more when you impart information than when you listen, you need to develop an awareness of your voice and body as delivery tools. Your voice messages should support your verbal messages by being easily audible, clearly articulated, at a pleasing level of pitch, with good use of emphasis, and at a comfortable speech rate for clients to learn from you. Body messages that support your verbal messages include relaxed posture, good use of gaze and eye contact, and gestures that emphasize your main points.

Consider using audiovisual aids to put your message across. For example, the structure of a presentation will be clearer if written on the whiteboard than if just spoken. Other audiovisual aids you could use include flipcharts, training manuals, handouts, and audio cassettes and videotapes. Beginning helpers especially are encouraged to practise putting content and delivery together. You may already possess good listening skills, so that clients want to talk to you; work on developing equally good sender skills so that clients want to hear from you.

DEMONSTRATING SKILLS

When training clients in applied lifeskills, add *show* to *tell*. 'Learning from modelling' is another term for 'learning from demonstration'. One of the main ways that clients learn is from hearing and observing performances of targeted skills. Such performances can demonstrate thinking skills, action skills, or action skills with accompanying self-instructions.

Who demonstrates? Very frequently, helpers demonstrate skills both as part of initial presentations and when subsequently coaching and rehearsing clients. However, clients can be asked to demonstrate skills for themselves, for instance, clients can make up cassettes of themselves using specific thinking skills competently. When recorded material is used – for instance, training videos or cassettes – third parties such as actors may demonstrate skills. Also, puppets and cartoon characters may be used as demonstrators.

Demonstrations may be written, live, recorded or visualized. Frequently, helpers demonstrate the same skill using more than one of these methods.

Written demonstration

Written demonstrations may be printed in books, training manuals and handouts. In addition, helpers can demonstrate material during sessions on whiteboards or notepads. Here written demonstration and live demonstration overlap. Thinking skills especially lend themselves to being demonstrated on the printed page and whiteboard. Advantages of printed demonstrations are that they can be easily stored and retrieved by helpers and clients, written examples can introduce homework assignments, for example, if training shy clients in the calming and coaching elements of coping self-talk, you could provide written demonstrations of coping self-talk statements for before, during and after a specific social situation – say, a party. Then you can ask clients to make up their own coping self-talk statements. Below I provide written demonstrations of such statements:

Before the party
'Calm down. I can think of some things to talk about before I go.'

During the party
'Relax. I can disclose something of myself as well as listen to others.'

After the party
'I used my self-talk skills and they helped me to feel more in control.'

Live demonstration

In individual helping, most demonstrations are probably live, because live demonstration has the advantage of here-and-now communication, and you can easily demonstrate appropriate voice and body messages. Flexibility is another advantage, as you can tailor-make demonstrations to specific situations that clients find problematic. Also, when coaching clients, you can use live demonstrations to provide feedback and make suggestions. Live demonstrations need not be restricted to helping sessions, for example, clients can be asked to observe in their daily lives people who are good and, possibly, poor models of targeted skills. A disadvantage of live demonstrations is that clients have no copies to listen to or watch on their own.

Recorded demonstration

Recorded demonstrations can be on films, audio cassettes and videotapes. Films are unlikely to be used during helping sessions because they are cumbersome to show, but clients might be asked to watch films demonstrating targeted skills outside sessions.

Audio cassettes are particularly useful for demonstrating thinking skills. Initially, provide the demonstrations yourself; later on, you can arrange for clients to make their own demonstration cassettes so that they get their own voices, rather than your voice, in their heads. To develop targeted skills as self-helping skills, clients need to listen repeatedly to cassette demonstrations. If possible, use highly sensitive recording equipment with little motor noise and background hiss. Also, rehearse and remake recordings until they are good, because clients resist listening to poor-quality cassette demonstrations.

Videotapes have the great advantage of showing body messages as well as verbal and voice messages. Consequently, videotapes are much better than audio cassettes for demonstrating action skills. You may know of commercial videotapes that demonstrate the skills you wish to train; otherwise you need to make your own. During helping sessions you can videotape live demonstrations by you, for instance, of how to deal with people whom clients find difficult. If you work repeatedly with clients with the same skills weaknesses – for instance, parents making aggressive requests to children – it may be worth developing your own demonstration videotapes. You require many of the skills of film directors when making such videotapes, including checking scripts, rehearsing actors and retaking passages as necessary.

Visualized demonstration

Visualized demonstration entails getting clients to imagine competent performances of targeted skills. For instance, clients who need to develop specific verbal, voice and body message interview skills can be relaxed and told to imagine themselves or others using the targeted skills. Visualized demonstration has the advantage of flexibility in both the range of scenes that you can depict and the instructions you can provide. Whether or not visualized demonstrations are used during helping sessions, clients can incorporate them into homework. A disadvantage of visualized demonstration is that some clients experience difficulty imagining scenes. Also, since clients never actually see targeted skills demonstrated, they may imagine the wrong things.

Demonstrator skills

Think through how best to incorporate demonstrations into tell, show and do sequences. Frequently, clients learn skills better if you combine methods of demonstrating, for example, live audio-cassette and written demonstration of the same thinking skills. Think through the level of competence of demonstrators. It is preferable to show demonstrators overcoming difficulties rather than being perfect all along. Also, consider whether to show how not to use targeted skills as well as how to use them. Often negative demonstrations can highlight skills you teach in positive demonstrations, but you need to ensure that the major emphasis is always on correct rather than incorrect use of skills.

Cue clients as to what to look out for in demonstrations. Consider what commentaries you need to provide during demonstrations and what summaries at the end. Check clients' learning, for instance, you can ask them to summarize the main learning points of the demonstration. Even better is to get them to demonstrate the skill they have just observed.

COACHING SKILLS

Though it may seem obvious, it is essential that helpers observe clients performing targeted skills. Many beginning helpers describe and even demonstrate skills, but then omit to coach clients in them. Following are some helper skills for coaching clients in targeted skills.

Use client-centred coaching

Think of your objective as training clients to be their own coaches. How best can you develop their skills at this? If you are very didactic, the emphasis is on their following your instructions; however, self-helping requires that they follow their own instructions. Consequently, coach in a way that develops their skills of assuming responsibility for their learning. Use supportive relationship skills to identify difficulties, fears and resistances to enacting skills both inside and outside helping. Make clients active participants in skills learning. For instance, after demonstrations you might say, 'Now you have observed that demonstration of _____ skill [specify skill], what have you learned that is relevant to your situation?'. Also, after clients perform skills, get them to assess how they did before you give them feedback.

Emphasize self-instruction

In your initial presentations and demonstrations, provide clear instructions for performing targeted skills. As necessary, when coaching, give further specific instructions, tips and prompts. However, coaching should always emphasize ways in which clients can help themselves, so aim to lessen your input and encourage clients to give themselves the instructions, tips and prompts.

Break learning tasks down

An issue in demonstrating and coaching is how much material to focus on at any one time. Frequently, you need to break learning tasks down. For instance, when coaching parents to make assertive requests to children, you might coach verbal messages first, then voice messages, then body messages, and then how to put all the skills together. Often, you need to coach clients in easier tasks before moving on to more difficult ones. Also, clients may require many trials before becoming proficient, so avoid moving on to new material too soon.

Use behaviour rehearsal and role play

Behaviour rehearsal and role play are not necessarily synonymous. For instance, clients may rehearse thinking skills and some action skills, such as relaxation, on their own. Role plays are especially useful for rehearsing action skills. Behaviour rehearsal and role-play skills are covered in more detail in Chapter 14.

Use feedback skills

Feedback is an important part of helping, as clients need to know how they get on and how they might improve their skills. Following are some feedback considerations:

- *Encourage client feedback.* At the risk of repeating myself, you need to encourage clients to assess themselves and provide their own feedback. Your feedback is also valuable, since you are a knowledgeable and neutral observer. However, get clients doing much of the work.

- *Give 'I'-statement feedback.* When giving feedback, use 'I' statements, for example, instead of, 'Your body posture was too tense', you might say, 'I thought your body posture was too tense', or 'I experienced your body posture as too tense.' Unlike 'You'-statement feedback, 'I'-statement feedback encourages clients to evaluate what you say about their performance. As such, it is more in keeping with imparting self-helping skills.

- *Be specific.* Feedback should always be specific. For instance, in the previous example you could specify why you considered the client's body posture too tense – shoulder blades pressed back, tight stomach, lack of movement and so on.

- *Demonstrate feedback.* As well as telling clients how you react to their performances, you can demonstrate how they come across. In the above example, you could demonstrate the client's shoulder blades presed back, tight stomach, lack of movement and so on.

- *Use confirmatory feedback.* Confirmatory feedback acknowledges correct behaviours, whereas corrective feedback focuses on altering incorrect behaviours. Tell clients what they do right and not just what they do wrong. Confirmatory feedback provides the emotional climate in which clients are more likely to listen to corrective feedback. Many clients are in helping because they have received too much corrective feedback in the past.

- *Consider audiovisual feedback.* Clients can learn much from listening to cassette recordings of how they use both thinking skills and verbal and voice messages. Videotape feedback can be very effective in showing clients the weaknesses and strengths of their body messages. Audiovisual feedback has the advantage of providing actual evidence of how clients perform, as well as lending itself to client self-evaluation.

- *Offer rewards.* However well or poorly clients perform, show attentiveness and interest through good use of verbal, voice and body messages. Ideally, clients find it rewarding to perform targeted behaviours well. However, you can also reward them for good use of skills, and giving confirmatory feedback is one way to do this. Saying 'Good' or 'Well done' is another way. Nonverbal rewards include head nods, smiles and even pats on the back. However, beware of getting clients dependent on your rewards rather than rewarding themselves or, even better, obtaining rewarding outcomes from using their skills in real life.

ASSIGNING-HOMEWORK SKILLS

The 'do' component of a tell, show, do sequence can include between-session homework. Some clients prefer words like 'assignments' or 'activities' to homework, since homework reminds them too much of school. Reasons for encouraging homework include speeding up learning, practising skills in real life, and finding out about difficulties in implementing skills.

One of the biggest problems with homework is that often clients fail to do it. Develop skills of making it easier for clients to comply. Following are some skills of increasing the likelihood of compliance.

Make a transition statement

Helpers can explain the importance of homework. In earlier structuring statements, you may have signalled that towards the end of sessions you will discuss using between-session time for homework. After you have coached clients in a skill, you can again raise the possibility of homework. Below is an example of a transition statement that provides a bridge from coaching to setting homework and explains why homework is important:

> Bronwyn, we're coming to the end of our session. For the past 10 minutes or so I've been coaching you in the skill of _____ [specify which skill]. However, learning any new skill properly requires work and practice. I think that you will get more benefit from our sessions if we can negotiate some between-session assignments. Then, near the start of our next session, we can review how you got on and, if necessary, work on difficulties. Do you have any problems with the idea of doing some homework?

Negotiate homework

Allow clients to participate actively in decisions about the amount and content of homework. Following are some characteristics likely to enhance clients' willingness to do homework:

- *Is perceived as relevant.* When setting homework, guard against being too helper-centred. Clients may fail to see the relevance of some homework suggestions. Sometimes clients' reservations are overcome by clarifying what you mean, while on other occasions clients may be clear, but see your homework suggestions as a partial or total waste of time. Asking clients to suggest homework assignments is one way to stay relevant.
- *Consolidates earlier learning.* If homework is a logical extension of the skills presented, demonstrated and coached in sessions, clients have a start in knowing what to do. All tasks should be of an appropriate level of difficulty.
- *Possesses clear requirements.* Clients need to have precise instructions, and one way to ensure this is to write them down. If any monitoring logs or worksheets are required, provide them yourself.
- *Is a realistic amount.* Clients need to make a commitment to doing homework. Negotiate with clients how much they are prepared to do, and encourage them to view doing homework assignments as fulfilling learning contracts with themselves.
- *Difficulties are anticipated.* Discuss with clients any difficulties they may have in completing homework, for instance, lack of support. Try to develop strategies for handling anticipated difficulties.
- *Rewards are possible.* Clients are more likely to do homework if there are some rewards attached to doing it. The best rewards are positive outcomes from using targeted skills. Clients' persistence may be increased if you teach them the difference between an outcome success (getting what they want) and a process success (using their skills well). They can still be successful even though they may not get everything they want.
- *Progress reviews are signalled.* Always check how clients have fared doing homework assignments. If you do not check on their progress, you give clients the message that complying with homework assignments is unimportant.

ACTIVITIES

1. Give an initial presentation of a skill or subskill to a partner who acts as a client. Focus on:

managing speech anxiety;
preparing clear content;
using appropriate audiovisual aids;
sending effective verbal, voice and body messages.
Afterwards, discuss and reverse roles.

2. Either on your own or with a partner, demonstrate one thinking skill and one action skill. For each skill, use at least two of the following methods of demonstrating: written, live, recorded and visualized.

3. Work with a partner and conduct a helping session in which you present, demonstrate, coach and assign homework for a targeted skill of importance to him or her. Aftwards, discuss and reverse roles.

THIRTEEN

How to focus
on thinking skills

Our life is what our thoughts make it.
Marcus Aurelius

This chapter focuses on how to intervene to attain working goals for each of the thinking skills discussed in Chapter 7. A major assumption of lifeskills helping is the *repetition phenonemon* – that clients' problems tend to recur. The repetition phenomenon's main cause is that clients remain ineffective in how they think. If you assist clients to think about how they think, you enhance their capacity to influence how they feel and act. Working with thinking is fundamental to helping clients experience, express and manage feelings. Also, thoughts and feelings tend to be the precursors of action. Developing thinking skills can remove blocks and inhibitions to action. Furthermore, good thinking skills can prevent self-defeating actions and fashion effective ones.

OFFER A SUPPORTIVE RELATIONSHIP AND ATTEND TO FEELINGS

When intervening to develop clients' thinking skills, it is essential that you offer supportive helping relationships. The desired helper–client relationship is one of mutual collaboration in pursuit of working goals. Safe and trusting emotional climates increase the likelihood of clients being honest with themselves and you. The more clients feel you are sensitive to their feelings and vulnerabilities, the more motivated they will be to work on emotionally crippling thinking weaknesses. Clients may require considerable support when they start distinguishing their thinking from what and how they have been taught to think. Assist clients in assessing and articulating their own thoughts, despite the pain and guilt this may cause. However, remain sensitive to how threatening certain topics are and be mindful of clients' defences and resistances.

Clients need to feel that thinking-skills working goals are emotionally valid for them. Tune into and check what goals and interventions feel right. Also, when clients learn new skills, support and encourage them at all stages – presentation, demonstration, coaching and homework. Instances in which they may feel insecure include recognizing past mistakes, uncertainty about understanding skills properly, being asked to demonstrate skills, and revealing homework difficulties. You are not only their coach but their companion, so you require good inner- and outer-game skills yourself to work with clients' inner-game skills.

GIVE REASONS FOR FOCUSING ON THINKING

When redefining problems and stating working goals, you can suggest some reasons for focusing on thinking skills. Later, when starting to intervene to attain a specific thinking-skills working goal, you can offer some reasons why it is important. Here is a brief introductory statement given to Elizabeth, a separated woman with two university-age children, who avoids discussing with Frank, her husband, his not paying his share of the children's university expenses. Developing Elizabeth's coping self-talk is the targeted thinking skill:

> Elizabeth, we agreed to spend part of this session looking at how you can use coping self-talk to combat avoiding difficult issues with Frank. Right now he is not paying his share of Tom and Nancy's university expenses. In the past you've got very agitated and lectured him aggressively. When that's happened, Frank looks pained and then fails to change. If we look at what's happening in the STC framework, where S is the situation,

T your thoughts, and C the consequences, you seem to say many negative things to yourself at T – for instance, 'I'm helpless', and, 'He will win anyway' – that have the consequences of increasing your anxiety and lowering your performance. Let's continue identifying some of your main negative self-talk sentences. Then we can work to replace them with calming and coaching statements that should assist you to cope better when confronting Frank. Later, we can work on some action skills too.

In your statement of working goals, you probably targeted more than one thinking skill. You may work on other targeted skills concurrently or one at a time. Often, in the same session, you will work with more than one thinking skill.

OWNING RESPONSIBILITY FOR CHOOSING

You can assist clients in becoming more aware that they are always choosers in their lives. Sometimes clients require more fundamental work focused on assisting them in experiencing their feelings more fully prior to being able to become more aware of their 'choice-ability'. Following are some suggestions for helping clients become more responsible for their choices:

- *Tell them.* You can raise some clients' awareness that they are always choosers by telling them. Even choosing inaction involves choice. Emphasize that clients are responsible not only for their actions, but for their thoughts and feelings. You may need to explain further how clients can choose how they think and that how they think influences how they feel.
- *Encourage choice language.* Clients may be poor at saying 'I think' or 'I feel'. If so, encourage them to use 'I' messages that locate the source of their thoughts and feelings in themselves. Encourage use of verbs that acknowledge choice, for instance, 'I won't', instead of, 'I can't'. You can also challenge static self-labelling, for example, 'I'm no good with men/women', rather than, 'I choose to be no good with men/women.' Also, you can challenge statements like, 'I had no choice but to . . .'.

- *Ask choice questions.* In many situations, clients may be insufficiently aware that they have a range of choices. You can try and broaden their horizons by questions like, 'What were/are your choices in how to act?' or 'What were/are your choices in how to think?'
- *Encourage clients to visualize opposites.* Sometimes clients get insight into their mental rigidities by being encouraged to explore opposite ways of thinking, feeling and acting. For instance, clients who are in serious conflicts can be asked to imagine themselves going out of their way to make their opponents happy, and how they might react. Clients with long-standing resentments can be asked to imagine themselves saying they forgive the other persons involved.
- *Confront passivity and externalizing.* You may need to challenge clients with the observation that, by being passive, they choose any resulting negative consequences. Some clients do little to change their lives because, in varying degrees, they externalize responsibility for their feelings, thoughts and actions on to others, for instance, by playing victim and martyr roles. You require both confronting and supportive relationship skills to assist such clients to examine their own behaviour and choices.
- *Increase death awareness.* Many people experience difficulty in being open and honest with themselves and others that their lives are finite. Some clients may gain increased awareness of the value of life from gaining increased awareness of the certainty of death. You can encourage clients to talk about their experiences of death and dying and their thoughts about their own deaths. Also, they can share how they wish to be remembered.

USING COPING SELF-TALK

Coping self-talk is a useful thinking skills that clients can use to manage many feelings, for example, anger, stress, anxiety, pain and shyness. Clients can also use coping self-talk to manage specific situations, for example, dealings with potentially hostile people, interviews, giving public talks and writing essays. Coping self-talk has also been used to enhance adult creativity and curb children's impulsiveness.

Following are steps in how to train clients in coping self-talk. Here the focus is more on content than on training methods.

Step 1 Introduce and raise awareness of self-talk

State clearly to clients that you are going to focus on attaining their working goal of developing better coping self-talk skills. Check how aware they are of how they engage in an internal dialogue all of their waking hours. If necessary, explain this to them. You can also get clients to do the exercise of closing their eyes for 30 seconds, trying to think of nothing, and then reporting how they got on.

Step 2 Identify current negative self-talk and its consequences

Put a specific situation into the STC situation (situation–thoughts–consequences) framework. With a mixture of supportive relationship skills and probes, assist clients to identify their negative self-talk statements at T and their consequences at C for how they feel and act. As appropriate, demonstrate negative self-talk.

Step 3 Present calming and coaching dimensions of coping self-talk

Calming and coaching statements tend to be interspersed in coping self-talk. Examples of calming statements are, 'Stay cool', 'Calm down', 'Take it easy', 'Relax', and 'Breathe slowly and regularly.' Coaching statements give clients instructions in the specific tasks they need to perform. Coping self-talk may be before, during or after specific situations, such as a job interview. Following are examples:

- *Before the interview:* 'Calm down. Just think how I can best prepare for the interview.'
- *During the interview:* 'Relax. Answer the questions that are asked and do not talk for too long.'
- *After the interview:* 'Take it easy. I used my coping self-talk skills and felt less anxious.'

Step 4 Relate coping self-talk to action

Assist clients in relating coping self-talk to action. Help them identify and work on specific action skills for managing situations better. Also, encourage clients to rehearse and then practise their coping self-talk skills and action skills in real life.

Step 5 Emphasize self-helping

Assist clients in retaining and using their coping self-talk. Get them to write it down on reminder cards and practise it daily for a set period. Also, encourage them to use it when necessary.

CHOOSING REALISTIC PERSONAL RULES

Personal rules provide standards for people to judge their own and others' behaviour. Sometimes these rules are realistic and based on clients' own experiencing of life; on other occasions, and in varying degrees, these rules are unrealistic and based on internalizations of others' standards. Albert Ellis, the originator of rational-emotive therapy, considers that all clients possess irrational beliefs or rules that lead to unwanted feelings and actions. Working with unrealistic rules is one of the most common ways that helpers intervene to develop clients' thinking skills. Following are some steps for training clients in how to choose realistic personal rules.

Step 1 Introduce and raise awareness of personal rules

Articulate clearly to clients that you are about to assist them in attaining their working goal of developing realistic personal-rules skills. Explore how aware they are of the fact that they possess numerous personal rules, some of which are realistic and others possibly unrealistic.

Step 2 Identify current unrealistic rules and their consequences

As appropriate, include either the PTC (problem–thoughts–consequences) or the STC (situation–thoughts–consequences) framework. Within one of these frameworks, assist clients in identifying one or more central unrealistic rules. For example, Bernie is a lecturer in psychiatric nursing:

S Despite thinking Bernie is competent, his class do not overtly appreciate his teaching.

T I *must* always have students' approval.

C Feelings consequences: hurt, mild depression and anger. Action consequences: sarcastic verbal messages and some withdrawal from students.

Teach clients the following cues that they may possess unrealistic rules:

- *Inappropriate language.* Unrealistic rules tend to be over-generalizations characterized by words like 'must', 'ought', 'should' and 'have to'.
- *Inappropriate feelings.* Seeming over-reactions in terms of either intense feelings or persistent negative feelings signal the possibility of unrealistic rules.
- *Inappropriate actions.* Actions that are self-defeating clearly signal that clients may possess unrealistic rules.
- *Inappropriate predictions.* Predictions of catastrophic outcomes – for instance, 'If I don't pass my exams, everyone will despise me' – are a further cue.

Step 3 Dispute unrealistic rules

Assist clients to develop skills of disputing or challenging their unrealistic rules. Take the earlier example of Bernie, whose unrealistic personal rule was, 'I must always have students' approval.' Following are examples of questions that you might ask Bernie or he might ask himself to check the logic of how he thinks:

- 'What evidence is there that my students do not approve of me?'
- 'Does every student have to approve of me to make me a good lecturer?'
- 'Do I have a double standard in that I evaluate how students react to my teaching more harshly than if other lecturers got the same reaction?'
- 'Did I always show appreciation to my lecturers?'

Make clients aware that they need to dispute the same unrealistic rules again and again.

Step 4 Reformulate unrealistic into more realistic rules

Help clients to understand some of the main characteristics of realistic rules, for example, expressing preferences rather than demands, emphasizing coping rather than mastery, avoiding perfectionism, and being based on their own valuing process rather than 'hand-me-downs' from others.

When training clients in how to reformulate their rules, get them doing much of the work. Also, use language that has meaning for them. Following is Bernie's reformulated rule:

Unrealistic personal rule: 'I must always have students' approval.'

Realistic personal rule: 'Though I would prefer to be liked by students, what is more important is that I teach well and they learn something of value from me.'

Step 5 Encourage clients to change actions along with reformulated rules

An important proof of the effectiveness of clients' new rules is whether they help them to act more effectively. You may need to work on specific action skills as well. Encourage clients to use both their changed thinking and action skills outside of helping.

Step 6 Emphasize self-helping

Encourage clients to rehearse and practise their choosing-personal-rules skills. Reminder cards and cassettes of reformulated rules can assist in maintaining their skills.

CHOOSING HOW YOU PERCEIVE

American psychiatrist Aaron Beck's cognitive therapy heavily emphasizes assisting clients in perceiving themselves and others more accurately. Marital distress, anxiety and depression are some of the main problems in which distorted perceptions play a large part. Following are some steps to take in training clients to perceive more accurately:

Step 1 Introduce and raise awareness of choosing how to perceive

State clearly that you are about to assist clients in developing their skills of perceiving more accurately. If necessary, assist them to see that people have choices in how they perceive themselves and others, for instance, they can choose to perceive only positive or negative qualities. Also, make links between how they perceive and how they feel and act. You can encourage clients to monitor the perceptions surrounding unwanted feelings. For instance, Felicity keeps a monitoring log of when she gets angry, which has one column each for situation (including date and time), her feelings and her thoughts.

Step 2 Distinguish between fact and inference

Often clients treat their subjective perceptions as 'facts'. Assist them to see that facts are what objectively happens and inferences are any subjective perceptions that go beyond what objectively happened. That a teenage son leaves his room untidy is a fact; that his mother takes this as a sign that he does not love her is an inference. Perceiving accurately involves, as closely as possible, matching inferences to facts.

Step 3 Help clients become aware of errors in how they perceive

Assist clients in identifying any consistent errors in how they perceive. Such errors include tunnel vision, polarized or black-and-white thinking, over-generalizing, and projecting their own defects on to others. An error many clients possess in perceiving themselves is to over-emphasize their weaknesses and minimize their strengths.

Step 4 Generate and evaluate different perceptions

Help clients to develop skills of stopping and thinking before jumping to conclusions. Part of this process includes asking themselves if their inferences are realistic given the available facts. Encourage them to ask questions like, 'Where's the evidence to support my perception?' Clients need to develop skills of generating different perceptions. For instance, their first perception on hearing a loud bang may be, 'There is a burglar in the house', but different perceptions include, 'The bang is a door slamming', or, 'The bang is a ball breaking a window pane.' The clients need skills of evaluating which perception best fits the available facts.

Step 5 Emphasize self-helping

Encourage clients to see the relevance of the skill of perceiving accurately as a self-helping skill, not just for now, but for the future. Stress the need for continuing practice of their skills in choosing to perceive accurately.

ATTRIBUTING CAUSE ACCURATELY

Attributions are how clients assign the causes of what happens in their lives. Frequently, clients make attributional errors that interfere with their motivation and effectiveness. Take the example of the secretary, Lydia, who unwillingly keeps staying late when, at the last moment, her boss asks her to do extra work. When Lydia assigns the cause of her staying late to her boss, she is powerless to do anything about it. However, when Lydia also assigns the cause to insufficient assertion on her part, she empowers herself. Following are some steps in training clients to assign cause better.

Step 1 Introduce and raise awareness of attributing cause

Clearly articulate that you are now going to work with clients to develop their skills of attributing cause accurately. Mention the importance of how people assign cause to how they feel and act.

Step 2 Identify inaccurate attributions and their consequences

Help clients to identify attributions that have negative consequences for them. You can use the PTC or STC frameworks. Following are some possible misattributions in different areas:

- *Causes of problems:* 'It's my genes', 'It's my mental illness', 'It's my unfortunate past'.
- *Depressed feelings:* 'I am the cause of all negative events in my life', and, 'It is hopeless for me to try to improve my life.'
- *Relationship conflicts:* 'It's all your fault', and, 'You must change first.'

Step 3 Challenge inaccurate attributions

Assist clients in challenging inaccurate attributions. For instance, for the attribution that the cause of the problems is people's unfortunate pasts, you can assist clients in: (1) examining the accuracy of their perception that their pasts are wholly unfortunate; (2) assessing whether it is possible for people to rise above their pasts; and (3) distinguishing between acquiring problems, where they may have been relatively powerless, and maintaining problems, where they can now assume responsibility for change. In addition, you can encourage clients to conduct experiments that test their attributions, for example, a husband who tries behaving better towards his wife may discover that the attribution, 'It's all her fault', was inaccurate.

Step 4 Formulate more accurate attributions

Assist clients to make and remember accurate attributions of cause. For instance, in a relationship conflict, the husband's attribution, 'It's all my wife's fault', might be changed to, 'I have a responsibility to look at how my own behaviour may contribute to destructive conflicts and, where necessary, change it.'

Step 5 Relate changed attributions to action

Assist clients to develop skills of changing their actions in line with their changed attributions. For example, the husband who no longer makes the attribution that his distressed marriage is all his wife's fault may need to develop specific action skills, such as showing-appreciation skills.

Step 6 Emphasize self-helping

Assist clients in recognizing that holding on to changed attributions requires work and practice. Get them to write down changed attributions and to rehearse them daily.

PREDICTING REALISTICALLY

Virtually all clients' problems contain disorders of prediction. Clients with debilitating anxieties and depression tend to over-predict that life is dangerous and hopeless, respectively. All predictions about the future are inferences, since the future has yet to happen; however, you can assist many clients to make more accurate predictions. Following are some steps in how to train this skill.

Step 1 Introduce and raise awareness of predicting

Articulate to clients that you are now going to focus on developing their skills of predicting realistically. If necessary, emphasize to them that they continually make predictions of varying degrees of accuracy.

Step 2 Identify negative predictive styles and predictions

You can assist clients to become more aware of their predictive styles and their consequences. Do they predict risk inaccurately by either underestimating or overestimating bad consequences of their actions, or both? Do they predict reward inaccurately by either under-estimating or overestimating good consequences, or both? What are the specific unrealistic predictions they keep making?

Step 3 Develop skills to predict more realistically

Following are skills that clients can use to increase the accuracy of their predictions:

- *Generate and evaluate additional risks or rewards.* Clients may focus too much on either risks or rewards. If so, they may need to develop skills of taking a more balanced perspective.

- *Assess probability.* Clients may wrongly assign high probability to low-probability events or low probability to high-probability events. Encourage clients to make their inferences fit the facts as closely as possible.
- *Identify strengths and supports.* Clients may predict more realistically if they can acknowledge specific strengths they may possess for coping with situations. In addition, they may identify supportive people to help them attain goals.
- *Test reality.* Sometimes clients are in positions to test the realism of their predictions. For instance, Vera is a shy widow who thinks she will be rejected if she asks Arthur, whose wife died three months ago, over for tea. Vera can test the realism of her prediction by inviting Arthur.

Step 4 Emphasize self-helping

Clients can write down their unhelpful predictive styles and predictions as a reminder to avoid them. Emphasize the need to work hard on maintaining skills of predicting more realistically.

SETTING REALISTIC GOALS

Some clients require assistance in setting goals. Assuming they are not badly out of touch with their valuing process, you can train them in skills of realistically setting and clearly stating their goals.

Step 1 Introduce and raise awareness of goal setting

Clearly articulate that you are going to focus on developing clients' goal-setting skills. If necessary, supply reasons for the importance of goal setting.

Step 2 Identify current poor goal setting and its consequences

Assist clients to identify such errors as lack of goals, unrealistically high or low goals, and 'fuzzy' goals. Help clients to understand the consequences of their poor goal setting.

Step 3 State goals realistically and clearly

Make clients aware that effective goals:

- *reflect their values*;
- *are realistic*, for instance, adequately acknowledge both personal and external constraints. Sometimes you may need to introduce sub-goals that lead up to the ultimate goal;
- *are specific*, for instance, to study from 9.00 am to 10.00 a.m. on Mondays, Wednesdays and Fridays;
- *have a time frame*, for instance, in the above studying example, the time frame is starting immediately and continuing for the remainder of the term. Where appropriate, state goals for maintaining changes, for instance, losing five pounds in four weeks and then maintaining my lower weight for at least three months.

Step 4 Emphasize self-helping

Encourage clients to use goal-setting skills in their daily lives. Work through any difficulties they anticipate in setting realistic goals on their own during and after helping.

VISUALIZING SKILLS

Visual images are important to all clients. The PTC and STC frameworks require expanding to allow for visual images at T. Many clients' visual images contribute to their problems, for instance, feeling stressed, performing poorly or giving in to temptations. Since visualizing is used for different purposes, training clients in visualizing skills is not presented here as a series of steps.

Introduce and raise awareness of visualizing

Clearly state to clients that you are going to focus on the working goal of developing their visualizing skills. If necessary, make them more aware of the role of visualizing in sustaining their problems, for instance, you can use the PTC or STC frameworks and ask about their visual images at T. Check how good clients are at getting visual images – some are better than others.

Help clients use visualizing to relax

When clients visualize, for whatever purpose, it is preferable that they be relaxed. When specifically training clients in relaxation skills, visual imagery can be used independently of or in conjunction with muscular relaxation. Here I focus only on visual relaxation. Encourage clients to identify one or more favourite scenes where they feel very relaxed, for instance, lying on a beach. Then you can demonstrate how clients can instruct themselves in visual relaxation. Below is an example of what first you and then they might say:

> I'm lying on an uncrowded beach on a pleasant, sunny day, enjoying the sensations of warmth and a gentle breeze on my body. The sea is peacefully lapping the shore. I haven't a care in the world and enjoy the sensations of peace and calm, peace and calm, peace and calm.

Help clients use visualizing to attain goals

Clients can be assisted in visually rehearsing the use of targeted action skills in specific situations. They can also rehearse accompanying self-instructions. Following is an example:

> Khalid has the goal of assertively telling Stuart to stop calling him a 'wog', even though Stuart seems only to be joking. Khalid visually rehearses and instructs himself in the verbal, voice and body messages he needs to send, including how he might respond if Stuart either apologizes or becomes difficult.

Often clients are far too good at visualizing the worst. They need to be able to counteract this tendency by visualizing themselves behaving competently and succeeding. Even if things were to go wrong, clients can still visualize themselves coping effectively with adversity.

REALISTIC DECISION MAKING

Frequently, clients experience difficulty in making decisions. If so, they may require training in the skills of realistic decision making. Here I focus on two areas, awareness of decision-making styles and rational decision-making skills.

Awareness of decision-making styles

Assist clients in becoming aware of unhelpful decision-making styles, so that they can counteract them. Following are five potentially unhelpful styles of personal decision making:

1. *impulsive:* clients make decisions rapidly, without thinking them through;
2. *over-cautious:* clients worry too much and try too hard, sometimes to the point of indecision;
3. *avoiding:* clients handle decisions by avoiding either confronting or making them;
4. *conformist:* clients conform, to others' expectations;
5. *rebellious:* clients rebel against others' expectations.

Following are two potentially unhelpful styles of making joint decisions in relationships. A cooperative or collaborative style is preferable:

1. *Competitive.* Clients operate on an 'I win – you lose' basis. Their approach is basically aggressive.
2. *Compliant.* Clients always go along with or give in to the other person. Their approach is basically passive and unassertive.

Rational decision-making skills

Some clients require assistance in developing skills of making decisions systematically. Following is a seven-step framework for rational decision making within the context of two main stages. Clients can possess skills strengths and weaknesses at each stage.

Stage 1 Confronting and making the decision
Step 1 Confront the decision.
Step 2 Generate options and gather information about them.
Step 3 Assess the predicted consequences of options.
Step 4 Commit yourself to a decision.

Stage 2 Implementing and evaluating the decision
Step 5 Plan how to implement the decision.
Step 6 Implement the decision.
Step 7 Assess the consequences of implementation.

Assist clients in working through current decisions systematically. Focus on developing their skills rather than doing their work for them. For example, instead of saying, 'Your options seem to be . . .', you can ask, 'What are your options and what information do you require to assess them?'. Your objective is to help them make wisely not only this decision but future decisions.

ACTIVITIES

1. In the first activity of Chapter 7, you assessed your strengths and weaknesses in each of the following thinking skills:
    owning responsibility for choosing;
    using coping self-talk;
    choosing realistic personal rules;
    choosing to perceive accurately;
    attributing cause accurately;
    predicting realistically;
    setting realistic goals;
    visualizing skills;
    realistic decision making.
State a personal working goal of developing one of these thinking skills. Using the suggestions made in this chapter, train yourself to attain your working goal.

2. Work with a partner who acts as a client with a working goal of developing a specific thinking skill. Within the context of a supportive relationship, use speaking, demonstrating, coaching and assigning-homework skills to train him or her in the targeted skill. Aftwards, discuss and reverse roles.

You may repeat this exercise by training 'clients', and by being trained yourself, in other thinking skills.

FOURTEEN

How to develop action skills

Thinking is easy; action is difficult; to act in accordance with one's thoughts is the most difficult thing in the world.
J. W. Goethe

How effectively clients act is a major test of how effectively they think. It is no use having a good inner game if you have a poor outer game. Action skills consist of verbal, voice, body and touch messages, and of the messages clients send when not in direct contact with others, for instance, letters or gifts. One approach to action skills is to lessen and extinguish action-skills weaknesses. A second approach focuses on learning new action skills and developing existing action-skills strengths. Though lessening weaknesses and developing strengths overlap, here the focus is on attaining working goals by developing action skills strengths.

WHEN TO INTERVENE

Should helpers work with action skills first, thinking skills first, or both together?

Clients differ in their problems and in how they approach life. Reasons for focusing on action skills first include the fact that some clients find it easier to accept working on their observable behaviour than on how they think. Also, clients gain in confidence when changed actions produce desired results. For instance, depressed clients who attain simple goals may lose some of their hopelessness, which may lead to further actions. Reasons for focusing on thinking skills first include the fact that some clients are too scared to act until they think more effectively. Also, those in relationship conflicts may need to change their attributions that 'it's all his/her fault', to free them to act effectively. Frequently, you work with thinking and action skills together. For example, partners learning caring skills need to think in more caring ways as well as to show more caring behaviours.

In sum, there are no simple answers in whether to intervene with thinking skills or actions skills first. You must assess the circumstances of each client on their merits.

MANAGE CLIENTS' RESISTANCES

Clients may be reluctant about or resist working on action skills. Changing their public behaviour is something they may have avoided successfully for a long time. If you lay the groundwork thoroughly in the first three lifeskills helping stages, you lessen the likelihood of lack of commitment. Following are other skills to use in assisting clients in overcoming resistances.

- *Offer a supportive relationship.* Clients may resist working on action skills where they consider that helpers are not genuinely interested in them as persons. Support not only clients' in-session, but also their out-of-session learning. They can get discouraged at real or imagined setbacks.
- *Work through fears.* Clients may fear working on targeted action skills both inside and outside helping sessions. During sessions, they may be reluctant to participate in learning tasks, such as role plays; outside sessions, they may be terrified about the consequences of changing the way they behave, for instance, incurring the wrath of psychologically powerful people. Also, they may have various beliefs that get in the way of change, for instance, 'I'm weak if I make the first move.' Some clients fear the consequences of success even more than those of failure. Give them permission to discuss fears about developing action skills strengths and assist them to explore their realism.
- *Enlist client self-interest.* Help clients to see both the negative consequences of continuing with existing action-skills weaknesses and the positive consequences of developing skills strengths. You

can use the whiteboard and ask clients the advantages and disadvantages of change. Questions like, 'Where are your currrent skills getting you?', can highlight the need for change.

- *Arrange for reward.* Where possible, build in an easily attainable goal or sub-goal that enables clients to attain early success. Also, reward clients' efforts yourself with interest and attention and comments like, 'Well done.'
- *Use confronting skills.* At times you may need to challenge clients with their seeming inability to work hard to change their actions. Handle confrontations tactfully. They should lead to exploring difficulties in implementing action skills and, where possible, to rectifying them.

DEVELOP CLIENT SELF-MONITORING SKILLS

Systematic self-monitoring enables clients to become more aware of their thoughts, feelings and actions. Here the focus is mainly on recording actions. However, thoughts, feelings and actions are often recorded on the same monitoring log. Below are a couple of examples of clients monitoring their actions:

Melissa, aged 46, is learning progressive muscular relaxation. She keeps a monitoring log for each time she practises relaxation, including date, time for how long, what she did to relax, how relaxed she became and any difficulties experienced.

Edward, aged 31, is trying to improve his marriage. One of his working goals is to spend more time with his children, Joan, aged 5, and Chris, aged 3. He keeps a monitoring log of how much time he spend with the children and what he does with them.

Self-monitoring is useful at the start of, during and after helping. As well as increasing awareness, self-monitoring provides information for assessing change. However, the effects of self-monitoring as a treatment intervention on its own are often short-lived. Most often self-monitoring is combined with or part of other interventions.

Methods of self-monitoring

Following are some methods of self-monitoring:

- *Frequency charts.* Frequency charts illustrate how many times clients enact a specific behaviour in a given period. For instance, clients may keep frequency charts of how many cigarettes they smoke, their alcoholic consumption, and how many hours they spend studying. Such information may be tallied hourly and then totalled daily. Sometimes frequency charts have many categories. For instance, charts to monitor job-search activities might have the following categories: written application; phone application; letter enquiry; phone enquiry; cold canvass; approach to contact; employment centre visit; and interviews attended.
- *Stimulus, response and consequences logs.* You can assist clients to become more aware both of how they act and of the antecedents and consequences of their actions. Clients can fill out stimulus, response and consequences logs to monitor such information (see Figure 14.1).

Stimulus (What happened?)	Response (How I acted)	Consequences (What resulted?)

Figure 14.1 *A stimulus, response and consequences log*

- *Use-of-targeted-skills logs.* Both when initially assessing clients' action skills, and later, when checking on how they use their new skills, you can ask them to fill out use-of-targeted-skills logs. Clients can record each situation in which they used their targeted skills. An example of such a log is provided in Chapter 8 (Figure 8.1), with 'Situation' in the left-hand column and then, under 'How I acted', a column each for 'Verbal skills', 'Voice skills' and 'Body skills'.

Assist in client self-monitoring

Following are some ways that helpers can assist in clients' self-monitoring:

- *Offer reasons.* Explain how self-monitoring can contribute to clients attaining working goals. For instance, you can say, 'Collecting information about your use of verbal, voice and body skills in specific situations can show how well you use your skills and where you need to improve.'
- *Design and provide recording logs.* Design simple and clear recording logs for targeted skills. Provide logs yourself, so that they are designed correctly and clients do not have the extra effort of making them up.
- *Train clients in recording.* Make sure clients are clear not only what to record but how to record it. Check with clients that they know how to make the necessary discriminations to fill in monitoring logs. As appropriate, give further instructions.
- *Encourage clients to evaluate information.* Assist clients to assess the results of their frequency charts and self-monitoring logs. After helping ends, you will not be around to do this for them.

SEQUENCE GRADED TASKS

Frequently, it is desirable to take step-by-step approaches to training action skills. Such approaches entail sequencing graded tasks so that clients attain sub-goals prior to attaining ultimate goals. There are two main, yet overlapping, approaches to setting sub-goals:

- *Component skills as sub-goals.* Here you break a skill down into its component parts, for example, training in turn the verbal, voice and body components of saying 'no' to an unreasonable request, before putting all three together.
- *Graded outcomes as sub-goals.* Here you identify the use of targeted skills in successively more difficult situations, for instance, ranking situations for the above client to say 'no' with easier ones before more difficult ones.

Helper skills for graded tasks

Work with clients in sequencing graded tasks, and encourage them to be realistic about their starting points. When sequencing tasks, go at a comfortable pace for them. If the progression of tasks seems too steep, build in intermediate tasks. When clients perform tasks, encourage them to think of themselves as conducting personal experiments in which they can gain valuable information about themselves, since such an approach makes it easier to avoid feelings of failure. Many graded tasks are performed as homework assignments, so during sessions you can rehearse how to perform the tasks. Clients can also rehearse tasks outside sessions both in practice and by using visualizing. Coaching and rehearsal increase the likelihood of clients' successfully performing graded tasks. Always review progress. In collaboration with clients, sequence easier or more difficult tasks as necessary. Assist clients to own their successes and to attribute the cause of these successes to their use of targeted skills.

CONDUCT REHEARSALS AND ROLE PLAYS

Learning any new skill tends to require repeated performances of targeted behaviours. Initially, such performances are likely to be in the presence of helpers. However, rehearsals conducted inside helping should lead to rehearsals conducted outside, so that clients use between-session time to the best effect.

Methods of rehearsal

Following are different methods of rehearsing action skills:

- *Live rehearsal.* Live rehearsals do not necessarily entail role play. Clients can rehearse many action skills on their own, for instance, progressive muscular relaxation, public speaking and making assertive requests, among others. Clients can use aids in their live rehearsals. For instance, when rehearsing how to speak in public, clients can use mirrors and cassette recorders.
- *Role play.* In role plays, helpers play people in clients' lives. Examples of role plays include confronting a relationship conflict, showing appreciation to parents, and giving instructions assertively at work. Sometimes helpers and clients switch roles, which can give clients insight into how it feels to be the other person and show them how they come across. Helpers can rehearse clients in self-instructions that accompany action skills. For

instance, Jeff is a builder with a number of customers with unpaid bills; his helper rehearses him in what to say both to himself and his customers.

- *Visualized rehearsal.* Visualized rehearsals are usually performed as homework assignments. For instance, Jeff can practise in his imagination the targeted verbal, voice and body-message skills for asking specific customers to pay up. Also, Jeff can instruct himself as he visually rehearses his action skills.

Skills for conducting role plays

Take the case of Jeff, the builder with many outstanding accounts. How can you use role play to improve his skills in collecting bad debts?

- *Present a rationale.* Jeff is a very down-to-earth person. He finds the idea of role playing off-putting. To ease his anxiety and motivate him, you can offer reasons for his participating in role plays:

  Jeff, I think it would help you attain your goal of collecting your bad debts if we rehearsed by means of role-playing the verbal- and voice-message skills you require when following up your payment reminder letters with phone calls. We can also rehearse some skills to use if you then visit customers, including your body messages. Rehearsing skills here, where mistakes don't count, prepares you for the real thing.

- *Assess current action skills.* Go beyond getting Jeff to describe how he goes about collecting outstanding accounts, to get him to show you, by setting the scene and putting you in role for one or more assessment role plays. For instance, if he is showing you how he makes a phone call, he can describe the physical setting as if it is a stage set, whom he phones and how he or she behaves. Then you can role-play the telephone call. Also you can elicit what Jeff tells himself before, during and after phoning.

- *Formulate changed actions.* Assist Jeff to assess where his action-skills strengths and weaknesses are. Focusing on one situation at a time – for instance, a specific customer – develop new and better ways of using targeted action skills. Review alternative verbal messages he might send and how the customer might respond. Also, improve Jeff's voice message, for instance, speaking clearly and firmly and cutting out his 'uh-mms'.

- *Rehearse changed actions.* Get Jeff to summarize the targeted skills he will use in the role plays. Once you and Jeff are clear about your respective roles, perform one or more role plays. You may sequence graded tasks in your role plays, for instance, focusing on verbal phone messages first and then incorporating voice messages. Also, you can role-play different ways the customer might respond, for instance, being apologetic, evasive or belligerent. You can allow individual role plays to run their course; alternatively, you can intervene along the way to provide feedback and coach. As part of this feedback and coaching you may use role reversal, in which you play Jeff and Jeff plays his customer. You can also rehearse Jeff's thinking skills along with his action skills.

- *Process role plays.* Processing entails spending time discussing how the role plays went, assessing how well Jeff used targeted skills, summarizing learnings, and making plans to implement rehearsed skills outside helping. As a result of processing, you may decide to perform further role plays; however, if you are satisfied with Jeff's skills at making phone payment requests, then you may go through the cycle (assess, formulate changed actions, rehearse, and process) in regard to making follow-up visits to customers.

ENCOURAGE PERSONAL EXPERIMENTS

A good way of getting clients to use targeted skills outside helping is to encourage them to conduct personal experiments. In setting up personal experiments, you can focus on action skills alone, thinking skills alone, or both together. In conducting personal experiments, clients are practitioner-researchers testing hypotheses that generate 'findings' about how well they use targeted skills and their consequences. Viewing the trying out of skills in experimental terms has a number of advantages. First, it encourages clients to think of all their behaviour in terms of choices and consequences. Second, it allows clients to remain somewhat detached – if experiments do not work, they can examine reasons for this rather than think they have failed as persons. Third, because it is less risky, thinking in experimental terms makes it easier for clients to try new skills in real life. Fourth, by enhancing transfer of learning from inside to outside helping, the experimental approach assists clients to develop self-helping skills.

A six-step approach to personal experiments

There are six main steps in designing, conducting and evaluating action skills experiments. Each step is illustrated here in relation to Jeff, the builder whose overall goal is to collect all outstanding funds from his debtors. For the sake of simplicity, I focus only on action skills in this description:

1. *Assess.* Helpers and clients assess clients' action-skills strengths and weaknesses in problem situations. Jeff's helper explores his action skills in collecting unpaid bills by encouraging Jeff to talk about what he does, asking 'how' questions about how he and others behave, conducting an assessment role play, and asking Jeff to fill in an action-skills monitoring log in which he records his verbal, voice and body messages and their consequences for each time he contacts customers about unpaid bills.

2. *Formulate changed action skills.* As a result of assessments, helpers and clients work out how to use better action skills to attain overall goals. In Jeff's case, he and the helper decide to design an experiment around making phone calls to collect unpaid bills. They target: (a) the verbal-message skills of using 'I' statements and making simple, direct requests that are repeated as necessary; and (b) the voice-message skills of reasonable volume, firm tone, good use of emphasis and measured speech rate. Since this is a phone conversation experiment, no body-message skills are targeted.

3. *Make an 'If . . . then . . .' statement.* The 'If' part of the statement relates to clients rehearsing, practising and then using their changed action skills. The 'then' part of the statement indicates the specific consequences they predict will follow from using their changed action skills. Ensure that clients have this written down. For example, Jeff's overall goal is to collect his unpaid bills.
   If
   when I phone my three major debtors I use the following skills:
   verbal skills – 'I' statements and simple, direct requests that are repeated as necessary; and
   voice skills – reasonable volume, firm tone, good use of emphasis, and measured speech rate;

then (I predict that)
- (a) I will feel more confident when I phone;
- (b) my message will be conveyed unambiguously; and
- (c) I will get at least two definite commitments to pay me back in full by stipulated dates.

4. *Rehearse and practise.* Possibly using action-skills role plays, clients need to rehearse and practise changed action skills to have a reasonable chance of implementing them properly. Jeff's helper uses role plays to rehearse Jeff in the targeted verbal- and voice-message action skills. Jeff is also encouraged to use visualized rehearsal as part of homework.

5. *Try out changed action skills.* Clients implement changed action skills in actual problem situations. After an adequate amount of preparation, Jeff phones his three major debtors.

6. *Evaluate.* Clients record what happened in their try-outs and evaluate both how well they used their action skills and whether each of their predictions was confirmed or negated. When helpers next meet clients, they assist them in assessing the 'findings' of their experiments. Where appropriate, further experiments are conducted and clients undergo additional training in the same or other skills. To continue with the example, after each phone call, Jeff records and assesses how well he implemented his targeted action skills and their consequences. When they next meet, Jeff's helper conducts a review of the experiment.

TIMETABLE ACTIVITIES

Rightly used, timetables can assist clients in developing action skills. Following are some areas and skills for timetabling.

Areas for timetabling

Purposes for which a blank weekly timetable with days at the top and hours down the left-hand side may be used include the following:

- *Timetabling daily activities.* Helpers assist clients in timetabling what they are going to do during the day (sometimes called activity scheduling). Once clients gain in confidence, they can make their own activity schedules. Timetabling daily activities is extensively used with depressed clients.

- *Timetabling minimum goals.* Timetabling minimum goals is an approach to helping clients who engage in avoidance behaviour to get started. The idea is that if they can attain minimum goals, this will show them that they can positively influence their environments. An example of timetabling minimum goals is that of Alex, who becomes extremely anxious at the thought of studying. Together Alex and his helper set two half-hour study periods in the next week, being specific about time, task and place. Alex can do more studying beyond his minimum goals if he wishes.
- *Timetabling to create personal space.* Alex was an example of a client using timetabling to create work space. However, many clients require timetabling to create personal space for leisure and relating.
- *Timetabling to keep contracts.* Timetables may be used to clarify and keep contracts with others. Examples include teenagers contracting when they will do their share of household chores and working spouses agreeing when they will spend quality time with each other.
- *Timetabling homework.* Clients can timetable when they will do homework tasks, for instance, practising muscular relaxation.

Some skills for timetabling

Timetables are no cure-all. Helpers need to introduce them sensitively and explain their benefits, and always to be mindful of the pressures that timetabling can create for highly vulnerable clients – beware of being just an extra source of pressure. Some clients openly resist timetabling; others go along with it, but have little commitment to doing what they put down. Tune in to clients' resistances and attempt to work through them. Do not overdo timetabling, as some clients may use it as a way of avoiding action. At subsequent sessions, review progress, offer encouragement for any positive steps clients have taken, explore reasons why clients do not adhere to timetables and, if necessary, amend them. Also, work with any thinking-skills weaknesses – for instance, perfectionist tendencies – and action-skills weaknesses that contribute to non-adherence to timetables. At all stages, aim to help clients develop timetabling skills to use on their own after helping.

USE EXERCISES AND GAMES

Exercises are structured activities with specific learning purposes, whereas games are exercises that involve play. Exercises and games can target specific thinking skills, action skills, or action skills with accompanying self-instructions.

There are two main sources of exercises and games: using existing material or making up your own. A major source of existing exercises is the Pfeiffer, Jones and Goodstein *Developing Human Resources* annual sets. My books *Relating Skills* and *Effective Thinking Skills* contain exercises and thinksheets to build these skills, while my *Training Manual for Counselling and Helping Skills* consists of numerous exercises and experiments to develop your lifeskills helping skills.

Other people's exercises may be inappropriate for the clienteles and problems with which you work. You may be able to amend some of them to increase their relevance, but in other instances, you may decide to develop your own exercises. This may be especially cost-effective if you keep seeing clients with the same kinds of skills weaknesses.

Designing exercises and games

Some helpers allow themselves to be too dependent on others' material. You may need to perceive your own potential and take the risks of being creative. Following are some guidelines in designing exercises and games:

- *Set clear, specific and relevant goals.* Many beginning helpers have a tendency to set vague goals, but clients should be clear about skills or subskills targeted by the exercise. Emphasize practical, take-away skills. Exercises need be highly relevant to clients' concerns, otherwise they have little motivation to complete them.
- *Give clear instructions.* Specify the main learning points of the exercise, and provide written, step-by-step instructions. When training in applied skills, a highly systematic approach is important.
- *Demonstrate exercises.* Where possible, provide written demonstrations of targeted skills. When asking clients to do exercises, demonstrate how to do them and answer queries.
- *Provide answer sheets.* As a minimum, written exercise kits should contain goals, instructions, one or more examples, and correctly laid-out answer sheets for the purposes of the exercise.

- *Test and process exercises.* If possible, try out exercises in advance to see if they work. Also, process how clients react to exercises and assess their feedback. Where necessary, refine or even discard exercises.

USE AIDES AND IDENTIFY SUPPORTS

As helpers, you may use, and assist clients to use, third parties to help them develop action skills.

Use helper's aides

Helpers may use a variety of people in clients' home environments as aides. Following are examples:

- Teachers assist children who are learning friendship skills.
- Spouses assist each other in developing managing-anger skills.
- Peers offer support and practical assistance to students with eating problems.
- Supervisors assist disabled workers when they re-enter the workforce.
- Managers assist employees to develop better skills in coping with work stress.

Helpers need to take care to identify suitable people as aides. Always obtain the permission of adults and older children; with younger children, use your discretion. Sometimes you can involve aides in planning interventions, for instance, teachers and school counsellors can work together to develop tailor-made programmes for pupils with study difficulties. Where necessary, train aides in their roles so that they can carry them out competently. Keep in touch with aides to ensure they perform their functions as agreed, and allow them to share observations about both clients' progress and their roles in assisting clients. Consider carefully the best time to withdraw the assistance of aides and how to go about this. Aim to develop clients' skills of helping themselves rather than their continuing to receive assistance from aides.

Identify and use supports

Supports in this context are people in clients' home environments who can assist them to develop targeted skills. Many clients require the skills of identifying and using supports. Following are some examples:

- Students with study-skills weaknesses seek out sympathetic members of staff.
- Women or men wishing to become more emotionally independent seek out like-minded people.
- Bereaved people identify people who will genuinely allow them to share their grief.
- Parents of schizophrenic children seek out other parents in the same predicament.
- Young offenders identify friends who are likely to help keep them out of trouble rather than get them in it.

You can raise clients' awareness of the importance of support in their lives, and ask them to identify people who might support them to develop targeted skills. If names are not readily forthcoming, you can assist them in searching for suitable people. In addition, help clients to identify people who might contribute to maintaining their skills weaknesses. If possible, develop strategies for avoiding or standing up to such people.

Once clients identify supports, they still require the skills of using them. Sometimes clients are reluctant to share problems with others as they may think themselves weak for seeking support or fear rejection if they show vulnerability. Where possible, assist clients in working through such fears. With some clients, you may need to develop specific action skills for obtaining support so that they do not go about it the wrong way. Also, some clients need to learn how to support others as a means of getting support for themselves too.

ACTIVITIES

1. State a personal working goal of developing a specific action skill. Design a form to monitor your use of the action skill, and record your behaviour for at least 24 hours.

2. Develop the action skill you stated as a working goal and monitored in activity 1 by using one or more of the following skills:

    sequencing graded tasks;
    conducting rehearsals and role plays;
    conducting a personal experiment;
    timetabling activities;
    using an exercise or game;
    identifying and using supports.

3. Work with a partner who acts as a client with a working goal of developing a specific action skill. Within the context of a supportive relationship, use one or more of the skills listed in activity 2 to train him or her in the targeted skill. Afterwards, discuss and reverse roles.

    You may repeat this exercise by training 'clients', and by being trained yourself, in other action skills.

FIFTEEN

How to focus on feelings

There is only one universal passion: fear.
George Bernard Shaw

Focusing on feelings is fundamental to both living and helping. All clients' problems involve feelings in one way or another. Also, in every helping session, both clients' and helpers' feelings are prominent. This chapter builds on previous chapters by showing how to focus on feelings by intervening with clients' thinking skills and action skills.

HELPERS AS FEELINGS EDUCATORS

Helpers are feelings educators who work in three main areas: experiencing, expressing and managing feelings. Many clients require help in getting in touch with their feelings and underlying animal nature. Some are able to experience feelings but are poor at communicating them, while many clients struggle with managing unwanted feelings, such as excessive anger, anxiety or depression.

Helpers as feelings educators require tough minds and tender hearts. You can show your tender heart by using rewarding listening skills to communicate sensitive understanding of clients' emotional lives. An exquisite saying of Lao-Tse highlights the quality of listening to which I refer:

It is as though he [she] listened
and such listening as his [hers] enfolds us in a silence

in which at last we begin to hear
what we are meant to be.

Helpers are more effective if tough as well as tender. Frequently, in addition to rewarding listening skills, you require assessment and training skills. As psychological educators, you assist clients in using what distinguishes them from lower animals – their capacity for introspection and reasoning – to regulate and manage their animal natures. Feelings represent nature; they are not skills. Consequently, assist clients in acquiring feelings-related thinking and action skills to influence how they feel.

CLIENTS' RESPONSIBILITY FOR FEELINGS

Clients are responsible not only for their thoughts and actions, but for their feelings. Following are questions for clients to ask themselves:

- *Experiencing feelings:* 'How can I get more in touch with my feelings?', 'How can I strengthen my sense of self?', 'Where do my feelings come from?'
- *Expressing feelings:* 'How can I communicate my feelings more directly?', 'How can I share intimate feelings?'
- *Managing feelings:* 'How can I stop my anxiety getting out of hand in assessment situations?', 'How can I control my anger?'

You need to assist clients in seeing their choices in how they experience, express and manage feelings. All the above questions were posed in ways that assume clients' responsibility for helping themselves. Though adverse past and present experiences may influence how clients feel, do not collude in their tendencies to avoid responsibility for their feelings choices.

EXPERIENCING FEELINGS

Assisting clients to experience feelings has three dimensions. Clients require the ability to become *aware* of their significant sensations. In addition, they need to *explore* feelings and feelings trails to see where they may lead. Also, they require skills of *labelling* feelings accurately, including ambivalent and complex feelings.

Following are some interventions to assist clients in becoming more aware of, explore and label feelings.

Legitimize the importance of feelings

You can help some clients focus on feelings by explaining why this is important. How you do this depends on the circumstances of individual clients. Following are examples of statements for Jock, aged 17, who sees a career counsellor, for Mae Ling, aged 43, who sees an occupational health worker, and for Dominic, aged 29, who sees a marital counsellor:

> 'Jock, you've been talking a lot about what careers your parents want for you, but your heart doesn't seem to be in any of them. I'm interested in *your* feelings about *your* future. Your feelings can provide you with useful information about what might be right for you. Perhaps you need to develop better skills at listening to what you feel rather than being so dependent on what others think. Would you agree?'

> 'Mae Ling, you're a highly successful accountant, yet you feel at the end of your tether. You keep pushing yourself and wonder how long this can go on. You experience lots of stress symptoms: difficulty in sleeping, feeling faint, concentrating poorly, listlessness and depression. You seem burned out and even heading for a breakdown. For the sake of your health, productivity and happiness, it is essential that you develop better skills at listening to your body and feelings. What do you think?'

> 'Dominic, you get a lot of feedback from your wife that you are poor at acknowledging her feelings and expressing your own. You say you were raised in a family where nobody openly discussed feelings. Now it's difficult for you to know what you feel and you lack spontaneity. Intimate relationships require people to be in touch with their own and each other's feelings. Might I suggest that loosening up your feelings be an important focus of our work together?'

Use rewarding listening skills

In Chapter 4, I focused on skills for rewarding listening and offering supportive helping relationships. Again, I emphasize here the importance of rewarding listening, because the quality of your listening can provide clients with the safety and freedom to allow themselves to acknowledge wants, wishes and threatening material. If you are good at assisting their exploring, you enable them to delve wider and deeper into feelings and personal meanings. Also, if you are accurate in reflecting feelings, you help them to label their own feelings accurately. Always, show sensitivity to the pace at which individual clients are prepared to work.

Use feelings questions

Helpers can use questions that assist clients in experiencing and sharing feelings. However, when answering, a risk is that clients talk about rather than experience feelings, so keep clients focused on feelings rather than thoughts. Clients are less likely to go 'into their heads' if you intersperse reflective responses with questions. Feelings questions include:

'How do you feel right now?'
'How did you feel then?'
'How do you feel about that?'
'Can you describe your feelings more fully?'
'I'm wondering whether you're feeling . . . [specify feeling]?'

Confront inauthenticity

You can use how you experience clients as guides to how honest they are about feelings. Clients can wear masks, put up smoke-screens and send multiple messages rather than 'level' with themselves and you. One way of confronting them is to say something along the lines of, 'I get the impression that you are only telling me part of the story. Am I right?' Also, you can share observations about how clients may avoid authenticity in helping sessions, and probably elsewhere, for instance, by habits such as changing the subject and using humour. You can confront clients who appear to externalize their feelings on to others, for example, 'You say your Mum hates you, but I get the feeling you hate her too.' In addition, you can confront inconsistencies between verbal, voice and body messages, for example, 'You say you are not anxious discussing him, yet you look away and tap your fingers.'

Use role-play methods

Role plays can be powerful ways of allowing clients to experience, explore and label feelings. For many clients it is more difficult to 'stay in their heads' during and after role plays than if they are just talking about what happened. Though role plays are ostensibly focused on actions, they elicit feelings; for instance, clients who role-play fights with partners can get deeply in touch with the feelings they experienced during and after their fights. When processing role plays, assist clients in articulating and exploring the feelings and thoughts generated by them.

Train inner listening skills

You can train clients to be rewarding listeners to themselves, so that they can develop the self-helping skills of becoming more aware of, exploring and accurately labelling their feelings. Following are some considerations when training inner listening:

- *Offer reasons for focusing on inner listening.* Earlier in this chapter I provided suggestions for statements legitimizing the importance of focusing on feelings. Let clients know that there are steps they can take to listen to themselves better.
- *Emphasize creating sufficient time and psychological space.* Clients can give inner listening priority in their lives by creating times and finding quiet places to get in touch with themselves. In addition, clients can clear psychological space for themselves to assess feelings connected with specific problems or decisions.
- *Encourage 'going with the flow'.* Getting in touch with feelings is a process that takes time, as feelings emerge and, possibly, change form. Encourage clients to flow with feelings and not cut them off prematurely. They should try to understand the meaning of their feelings messages and to label them accurately. Clients may require

a number of inner-listening sessions to work through what they really feel and think about specific matters. You may help clients to understand the skill of 'going with the flow' if you demonstrate this by verbalizing your feelings and associated thoughts as you attempt to listen to yourself.

Focus on thinking skills

Often, the ways clients think influence their capacity to experience feelings. Following are illustrative thinking-skills weaknesses that block acknowledging and accurately experiencing feelings. Refer to Chapters 12 and 13 for how best to develop clients' thinking skills:

- *Owning responsibility for choosing.* Many clients inadequately acknowledge the extent to which they can choose how they feel.
- *Using coping self-talk.* Clients can enhance their capacity to access feelings by avoiding negative self-talk. Instead they can make calming statements like 'Stay calm' and 'Relax', and coaching statements like, 'Take my time to get in touch with how I truly feel.'
- *Choosing realistic personal rules.* Many clients have unrealistic rules that interfere with experiencing feelings. Following are some examples: 'Women should not acknowledge ambition', 'Men must not show sensitivity', 'Christians should turn the other cheek', and, 'It's unnatural to experience homosexual feelings.'
- *Choosing to perceive accurately.* Clients' perceptions heavily influence how they feel. Frequently, clients jump to conclusions that lead to negative feelings about self and others.
- *Attributing cause accurately.* Many clients externalize the cause of some of their feelings, for instance, 'He/she made me feel that way.' Also, clients make many attributional errors, for instance, depressed clients over-attributing the causes of negative events to themselves, and people in marital conflicts each placing all the blame on the other one.
- *Predicting realistically.* Unrealistic predictions lead to experiencing such feelings as excessive anxiety and a sense of hopelessness.
- *Setting realistic goals.* Lack of clear goals may lead to confusion. Unrealistically high goals can lead to anxiety and, if they are unattained, to depression.

- *Visualizing skills.* Negative visualizations can lead to feelings of tension and panic. Unnecessarily visualizing lack of success can contribute to unwanted anxiety and pessimism.

Encourage action

In most instances, clients need to act differently to feel better about themselves. Sometimes clients may never know what they truly feel until they act. For instance, clients may find it difficult to know how much they dislike any activity or person without first-hand knowledge. If successful, all the interventions mentioned in the previous chapter for developing clients' action skills should beneficially influence how they feel. For instance, if clients attain specific action skills goals, they become more confident about repeating their successes. The more clients are able to develop their action skills to attain goals, the stronger is likely to be their sense of identity and self-worth. Consequently, helpers require not only sensitivity to clients' feelings, but skills for helping them confront their avoidances and take effective actions.

EXPRESSING FEELINGS

Clients who have difficulty being aware of, exploring and accurately labelling feelings are also likely to have difficulty expressing them. Clients go public when they express feelings, and this can be very threatening. Some clients find virtually all feelings difficult to express; others have difficulty expressing particular feelings, such as anger, sexuality, confusion, vulnerability and grief. How well clients express feelings is also affected by the situations and people involved. The act of expressing feelings involves observable action skills. Nevertheless, how clients think influences whether and how well they develop and use their action skills.

Focus on thinking skills

Thinking-skills weaknesses interfering with appropriate expression of feelings overlaps with those blocking clients' experiencing of feelings. Following are some illustrations of why you may need to work with clients' thinking skills to support the development of their action skills. Again, refer to Chapters 12 and 13 for how to develop clients' thinking skills:

- *Owning responsibility for choosing.* Clients may inadequately assume responsibility for their choices in how they express feelings. You need to increase their 'choice-ability'.
- *Using coping self-talk.* Clients may use negative self-talk when expressing feelings, for instance, 'I am no good at it.' Also, they may fail to calm themselves down and coach themselves through how to express feelings effectively.
- *Choosing realistic personal and relationship rules.* Many personal and relationship rules interfere with expressing feeling appropriately. Illustrative personal rules are, 'I must have approval', and, 'I must not make mistakes.' Illustrative relationship rules are, 'We must never have conflict', and, 'We must always compete.'
- *Choosing to perceive accurately.* The degree to which clients misperceive themselves and others influences the degree to which they are likely to express feelings inappropriately. Also, clients require flexibility in perceiving various options for how to express feelings.
- *Attributing cause accurately.* Clients require the ability to take initiatives in expressing feelings rather than waiting for others to make the first move. Attributions – for instance, unjustified blame – heavily influence what feelings clients express and how they do it.
- *Predicting realistically.* Unrealistic predictions interfere with expression of feelings, for instance, shy clients may not take social initiatives because they over-predict both rejection and their inability to withstand rejection.
- *Setting realistic goals.* Clients need to set realistic goals in expressing feelings, for example, courting couples progressively revealing feelings rather than frightening themselves and each other with premature disclosures.
- *Visualizing skills.* Some clients are poor at visualizing both how to express feelings and what their positive and negative consequences may be.

Focus on action skills

Helpers can assist clients in developing action skills of expressing feelings. Refer to Chapters 12 and 14 for the skills of doing this. Always focus on voice and body messages as well as verbal messages. You may also focus on touch and action messages. Following is a case example:

> Sally Anne, aged 53, is the head of a claims department in an insurance company. Morale in her department has been low and Sally Anne has received feedback that she notices negatives but rarely praises positives. One of her working goals is to develop her showing–appreciation skills. Sally Anne and her helper consider the following possibilities:

- *Verbal messages:* saying things like, 'Thank you for your work', 'I appreciate what you've done', 'Good work', and 'Well done'.
- *Voice messages:* clear and firm voice, with emphasis on words like, 'Thank you', and 'I appreciate'.
- *Body message:* positive body messages such as good use of gaze and eye contact, and smiling.
- *Touch messages:* Sally Anne thinks both she and the staff might feel uncomfortable with touch messages, though occasionally a light touch on the arm or shoulder may be appropriate.
- *Action messages:* inviting colleagues to coffee or lunch, and sending notes of appreciation when work is particularly well done.

MANAGING FEELINGS

Many clients come for helping wanting release from feelings that impact negatively on themselves and others. Following are examples:

- Lucy, aged 11, is painfully shy, and wants to be less lonely.
- Boris, aged 32, has trouble controlling his anger both at home and at work.
- Arthur, aged 47, suffers from feelings of persistent depression and wants to get more involved in life.
- Vivien, aged 19, suffers from examination anxiety and fears it will wreck her chances of getting good grades.

Helpers need to work with both clients' thinking skills and their action skills to help them manage unwanted feelings. In practice, feelings tend to overlap and clients may be anxious, depressed and irritable. Also, clients' skills weaknesses can contribute to more than one negative feeling, for instance, perfectionist rules about achievement may contribute to anxiety and depression. Consequently, success in developing skills for handling one feeling will be likely to transfer to handling other feelings too. Here, rather than covering a range of feelings, anxiety is used as an example of how to assist clients in managing feelings.

Managing anxiety

All people, not just clients, suffer from various levels of debilitating anxiety. Sometimes their anxiety is chronic or persistent; sometimes it is acute or sharp. Anxiety is a normal survival mechanism that should signal realistic dangers. However, frequently clients are too vigilant and, rather than helping them, their anxieties work against them. A limited goal is to assist clients to develop skills to cope with difficult situations at tolerable levels of discomfort, whereas a much more ambitious goal is to assist clients to develop skills of virtually eliminating debilitating anxiety so that all that remains is helpful anxiety. An immediate goal is to minimize interference from clients' anxieties right here and now, in helping sessions.

Invariably, you need to focus on thinking skills when assisting clients in managing anxiety. For some clients, the combination of focusing on how they think and a supportive helping relationship may be sufficient to free them to use action skills latent in their repertoires. However, often clients' action-skills weaknesses both cause and result in anxiety. For example, poor reading, organization of study time, and revision skills may contribute to how anxious students feel about their state of preparation for exams. In turn, during exams, this anxiety contributes to poor test-taking skills, for example, not reading questions properly and allocating time poorly. Consequently, such clients need to develop relevant action skills and not just thinking skills.

Table 15.1 shows some common thinking skills for managing anxiety. The requisite action skills are more difficult to list since they vary with clients' problems, for instance, meeting people, writing essays, being interviewed, and coming to terms with death. Also, take into account each client's individual circumstances.

Table 15.1 *Illustrative thinking and action skills for managing anxiety*

Thinking skills	Action skills
Using coping self-talk	Skills required for specific situations
Possessing realistic personal rules	Relaxation skills
Perceiving others and self accurately	
Predicting realistically	
Setting realistic goals	
Using visualizing	

Following are details of the thinking skills:

- *Using coping self-talk.* Anxious clients engage in much negative self-talk. Their anxiety symptoms are signals for telling themselves that they cannot cope or do anything right. In social situations their self-talk may be about making fools of themselves. Often clients with panic disorders tell themselves that a vital system, such as their heart, may collapse.
- *Possessing realistic personal rules.* Anxious clients tend to have personal rules that engender both fear of failure and self-devaluation. Making perfectionist demands on self and others is a central characteristic of such rules.
- *Perceiving self and others accurately.* Anxious clients overemphasize the degree of threat in situations. They selectively perceive what might go wrong and insufficiently perceive what might go right, including their ability to cope and supportive people in their environments. Defensiveness, in which clients deny or distort threatening information, is another way that anxiety interferes with perception.

- *Predicting realistically.* Predictions of anxious clients exaggerate dangers and risks. Such clients worry about the future and their ability to cope with it.
- *Setting realistic goals.* Some anxious clients set goals that are too low, in order to avoid failing; some clients become anxious about their ability to achieve goals that are too high; and many clients overload themselves with goals and feel stressed and anxious as a result. The goals of some clients are realistically attainable when they manage anxiety better.
- *Using visualizing.* Most anxious clients experience negative visual images prior to and concurrent with anxiety attacks. Clients may possess poor visualizing skills for relaxing themselves and for rehearsing action skills.

Following are details of the action skills:

- *Skills required for specific situations.* Anxiety may be either a cause of poor action skills, or their consequence, or a mixture of the two. Some clients have good action skills, but have difficulty using them under pressure; other clients need to develop specific skills, for instance, listening to customers, learning to dance, giving pleasure to a sexual partner, policing an angry crowd and so on.
- *Relaxation skills.* Many anxious clients have poor relaxation skills. They engage in insufficient recreational activities, and may have poor muscular and mental relaxation skills.

Relaxation skills

Helpers can train clients in muscular and mental relaxation skills. Teach clients how to relax themselves rather than remaining dependent on you for relaxation instructions. Clients may use relaxation skills not only for managing specific anxieties, but for problems such as tension headaches, hypertension and insomnia. Relaxation skills can be used on their own or as part of more complex procedures, for instance, systematic desensitization. Possibly the simplest relaxation skill for clients is to use coping self-talk consisting of a calming instruction, 'Relax', followed by a coaching instruction, 'Breath slowly and regularly'. Other relaxation skills include the following:

PROGRESSIVE MUSCULAR RELAXATION SKILLS

Progressive muscular relaxation refers to the progressive cultivation of the relaxation response. Tell clients that the first step in physically relaxing themselves is to find a quiet, comfortable place. Progressive muscular relaxation involves clients in tensing and relaxing the following muscle groups: right hand and forearm; right biceps; left hand and forearm; left biceps; forehead; eyes, nose and upper cheeks; jaw and lower cheeks; neck and throat; chest and shoulders; stomach; right thigh; right calf; right foot; left thigh; left calf; and left foot.

You can demonstrate how clients should go through a five-step tension–relax cycle for each muscle group. These steps are: (1) *focus* attention on a particular muscle group; (2) *tense* the muscle group; (3) *hold* the tension for five to seven seconds; (4) *release* the tension in the muscle group; and (5) *relax* – spend 20 to 30 seconds focusing on letting go the tension and further relaxing the muscle group.

Inform clients that progressive muscular relaxation requires practice if they are to gain its full benefits. When learning, clients should practise daily for at least 15 minutes. In addition, clients can practise using muscular relaxation as a self-helping skill when preparing for specific situations, for instance, interviews or public talks. For their homework, either provide clients with existing relaxation cassettes or make them afresh. Later, coach them as they make their own self-instructional cassettes.

BRIEF MUSCULAR RELAXATION SKILLS

Brief muscular relaxation skills aim to induce deep relaxation with less time and effort. You may introduce such skills after progressive muscular relaxation, as they can save time both inside and outside helping sessions. Following are two methods:

1. *Sequential brief relaxation.* Here you count to ten, pausing every two numbers to instruct clients through the five-step relaxation cycle for four composite muscle groupings and then all muscle groupings together. For instance, 'One, two . . . focus on your leg and feet muscles . . . etc.; three, four . . . take a deep breath and focus on your chest shoulder and stomach muscles . . . etc.; five, six . . . focus on your face, neck and head muscles . . . etc.; seven,

eight . . . focus on your arm and hand muscles . . . etc.; nine, ten
. . . focus on all the muscles in your body . . . etc.' After they
receive instructions from you, clients need to be taught by you to
instruct themselves through this sequence.

2. *Simultaneous brief relaxation.* As in the final step of sequential
brief relaxation, clients tense all muscle groupings simultaneously.
Ask clients to take a deep breath, focus on each of the four
composite muscle groupings, tense all of them together, hold,
relax and release.

MENTAL RELAXATION SKILLS

Either in conjunction with or independently of muscular relaxation,
clients can visualize restful and calming scenes. Such a scene might be,
'lying in a lush green meadow, on a warm, sunny day, feeling a gentle
breeze, and watching the clouds drift by in the blue sky above'. As with
muscular relaxation skills, teach mental relaxation skills as self-helping
skills.

SYSTEMATIC DESENSITIZATION

Progressive muscular relaxation forms an important part of systematic
desensitization. This involves three elements: first, training clients in
progressive muscular relaxation; second, constructing hierarchies that
rank anxiety-evoking situations around themes, such as fear of heights
or of spiders, describing items so that clients can imagine them; and
third, asking clients, when relaxed, to imagine scenes from hierarchies,
starting with the least anxiety-evoking scene and progressively moving
on to more difficult scenes as clients become comfortable imagining
earlier scenes. Increasingly, helpers present systematic desensitization
as a self-control skill. They encourage clients who are experiencing
anxiety with specific items to relax and engage in coping self-talk. The
emphasis is on managing anxiety rather than on mastering it
altogether.

In vivo or real-life desensitization is a variation of systematic
desensitization. However, hierarchy items need to be readily available,
for instance, for someone afraid of heights, a tall building for
progressively going to higher floors.

USING MEDICATION

When assisting clients to manage feelings, helpers require familiarity with psychotropic drugs – drugs that act on the mind. If medication seems advisable, refer clients to physicians. If you are working with clients who are on medication, you may need to discuss appropriate dosages and side effects with physicians or look them up in reference sources, such as the latest edition of MIMS. All psychotropic drugs have possible toxic or unwanted side effects, for instance, even minor tranquillizers can affect some clients with drowsiness, lessened muscular coordination, lowered sex urge and dependency. If necessary, explore your own and clients' attitudes towards using drugs. Some clients resist any medication, where others treat it as a crutch. Aim for clients to become psychologically self-reliant in managing feelings. Though some clients may initially require medication, as helping progresses you may be able to wean them off drugs, possibly by smaller and less frequent doses. For quick-acting drugs, another option is to recommend that clients use them only in emergencies.

ACTIVITIES

1. Work with a partner who acts as a 'client' who has difficulty experiencing either his or her feelings in general or a specific feeling, for instance anger. Intervene to assist your client in experiencing feelings by using one or more of the following skills:
   legitimizing the importance of feelings;
   using rewarding listening skills;
   using feelings questions;
   confronting inauthenticity;
   using role-play methods;
   training in inner listening skills;
   focusing on thinking skills;
   encouraging action.
   Afterwards, discuss and reverse roles.
2. Work with a partner who acts as a 'client' with a working goal of expressing a specific feeling better. Within the context of a supportive relationship, intervene to assist your client to expressing his or her feeling better, by:

    (a) focusing on thinking skills, and then

    (b) focusing on action skills.

  Afterwards, discuss and reverse roles.

3. Work with a partner who acts as a 'client' who has difficulty managing a specific feeling. Redefine your client's problem in skills terms, state working goals and use one or more interventions to develop your clients' targeted skills.

    Afterwards, discuss and reverse roles.

SIXTEEN

How to consolidate self-helping skills

The toughest thing about success is that
you've got to keep on being a success.
Irving Berlin

Stage 5 of the lifeskills helping model looks not only at how to end helping, but at how to ensure that skills learned in helping do not end there (Figure 16.1). Following are examples of helping outcomes that have not lasted:

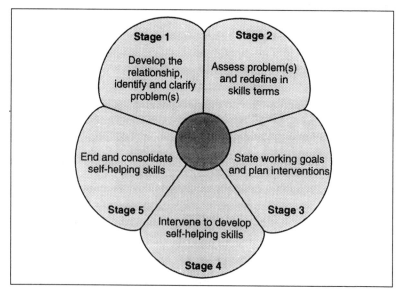

Figure 16.1   *Stage 5 End and consolidate self-helping skills*

Darren, aged 35, sought help from a weight-loss counsellor and by the end of three months had reduced his weight substantially. Three months further on, Darren is back to his old weight and eating habits.

Kathy, aged 25, came to helping worried that her marriage would break up due to the sharpness of her tongue. Kathy reported a long-standing problem of controlling her temper. During helping, Kathy's anger-management skills improved considerably. Once helping ended, she progressively went back to her old ways.

Always assume that it is hard for former clients to hold on to success. Throughout this book I use the term 'self-helping skills' to indicate the need to maintain and develop skills on a continuing basis. For most clients, what is really important in helping is what happens afterwards. First, they need to transfer skills learned in helping to outside. Then, after helping, despite setbacks and lapses, they need to maintain skills strengths. Also, where possible, clients should improve the way they perform targeted skills. Even in short-term helping, you can assist clients to hold on to their gains, and in longer-term helping, you have considerably more scope.

FOCUS ON THINKING SKILLS

When assisting clients to consolidate trained skills as self-helping skills, focus on how they think. Impart the lifeskills helping psychological education approach and language. Assist clients to view problems as sustained by learned skills weaknesses that can be unlearned and replaced with skills strengths. By emphasizing the word 'skills', you avoid lulling clients into thinking they are cured. Lifeskills are only for life if clients work to maintain them for life. If you provide truly elegant treatment, you move beyond treating specific problems and problematic skills weaknesses to educate clients to adopt a lifeskills approach to all situations in their lives. Following are some illustrations of how to focus on thinking skills to consolidate trained skills as self-helping skills:

- *Owning responsibility for choosing.* Emphasize the importance of clients choosing to maintain lifeskills.
- *Self-instructing.* Ensure that clients understand skills well enough to be able to instruct themselves in them. Where skills are complex, teach clients the main rules for carrying them out, for instance, communication rules for couples.
- *Using coping self-talk.* Clients can use coping self-talk when faced with 'hot' thinking connected with temptations such as food and high-risk sex. They can acknowledge the risk of lapsing, calm themselves down, and then coach themselves with specific instructions in what to do.
- *Possessing realistic rules.* Clients can develop realistic rules about maintaining skills. For example, unrealistic rules such as, 'Maintaining skills must be easy,' and 'I must never have lapses', can be identified, disputed and reformulated.
- *Perceiving accurately.* Clients can strengthen their ability to maintain changes if they perceive their successes accurately and do not exaggerate setbacks. Clients can avoid over-generalizing single lapses into permanent relapses. Unless clients perceive it as such, going backwards is not the same as staying backwards.
- *Attributing cause accurately.* Numerous attributional errors can interfere with maintaining gains, for instance, blaming others for failures and attributing successes to external factors rather than to personal effort, skill and willingness to take risks.
- *Predicting realistically.* Clients are more likely to retain targeted skills if they can accurately predict the gains of continuing to use them. Also, clients able to predict high-risk situations can develop strategies to deal with them.
- *Goal-setting skills.* Clients should always have the goal of at least maintaining end-of-helping skills levels. In conjunction with helpers, clients can set working goals for maintaining and developing targeted skills. Such skills-development goals should be specific, realistic and possess a time frame.
- *Using visualizing.* Clients can use visualizing to imagine the gains of maintaining skills strengths and the losses of reverting to skills weaknesses. In addition, clients can keep using visualized rehearsal to maintain targeted skills.
- *Using self-reward.* Clients can reward themselves for continuing using targeted skills, for instance, students maintaining studying

targets might reward themselves with CD purchases. Also, clients can verbally reward themselves for maintaining skills, for instance, 'Good. I hung in there and used my skills', 'Well done,' and, 'That shows I can keep doing it.'

FURTHER SKILLS FOR ENHANCING CONSOLIDATION

From helping's start, assume that clients will not hold on to trained skills. Your first challenge is how to stop premature termination, and your second is how to assist clients to maintain and develop skills after helping. Leaving the facing of such challenges to stage 5 of the lifeskills helping model is too late; effective helping has its endings built into its beginnings. In addition to focusing on thinking skills, following are suggestions for further skills to use in the first four stages of the DASIE model.

Stage 1 Develop the relationship, identify and clarify problem(s)

Below are some helper skills for consolidating clients' self-helping skills during stage 1:

- *Offer a supportive helping relationship.* This is important throughout helping, because clients who are feeling sensitively understood and supported are much more likely to listen to and learn from you.
- *Structure for maintenance.* Your first structuring statement may be a permission for clients to tell their stories. However, when making structuring comments later about how you work, use skills language and emphasize the importance of clients working hard to maintain skills after helping. Following is the kind of statement that helps dispel clients' beliefs in magic:

> 'There is no concept of cure in this approach. Even after helping, you're still going to have to work to retain your skills and their benefits.'

- *Develop self-monitoring skills.* Clients are more likely to retain skills if they can accurately monitor their use of them. From helping's start, assist clients in being systematic and accurate observers of their own behaviour.
- *Develop clients' clarifying-problems skills.* Assist clients to develop skills of breaking problems down into their component parts and collecting further information about the parts.

Stage 2 Assess problem(s) and redefine in skills terms

Helper skills for consolidating clients' self-helping skills during stage 2 include the following:

- *Develop clients' self-assessment skills.* Go beyond assisting clients in monitoring their behaviour to assisting them in making accurate assessments of the significance of this information for sustaining their problems.
- *Develop clients' skill at redefining problems in skills terms.* Let clients know why it is important to break problems down into thinking- and action-skills weaknesses. Draw them into the process as you redefine their problems. Especially in longer-term helping, you can give them practice at redefining emerging problems in skills terms rather than do it for them. Let clients know about any of their characteristic thinking-skills weaknesses that can reappear in other problems, for instance, unrealistic perfectionist rules and minimizing positive feedback.

Stage 3 State working goals and plan interventions

Following are some skills for enhancing consolidation of clients' skills during stage 3:

- *Develop clients' skills at stating working goals.* Clear initial statements of working goals make it easier for clients to develop skills during helping and maintain them afterwards. In longer-term helping you can coach clients in translating redefinitions of problems in skills terms into statements of working goals.
- *Plan interventions to enhance maintenance.* You can emphasize maintenance, when you both plan and deliver interventions, by focusing on self-instruction. In addition, plan to train skills

thoroughly, diversely and emphasizing real-life situations. Go beyond training skills to the points where clients initially change behaviour, to ensure that they over-learn them to assist in remembering them. Plan broad training that helps clients to respond flexibly to diverse situations. Focus presentations, demonstrations, coaching and homework on assisting clients in transferring targeted skills to real-life settings.

Stage 4 Intervene to develop self-helping skills

Helpers who deliver interventions well enhance the likelihood of clients maintaining targeted skills afterwards. Below are some further enhancing maintenance skills for stage 4:

- *Emphasize homework assignments.* Realistic homework assignments provide a bridge between learning and maintaining skills. Well-chosen homework assignments offer clients opportunities to develop skills progressively. Always review homework, both to assess progress and to identify difficulties and setbacks. Use helper skills such as role-playing to assist clients in overcoming difficulties identified in homework reviews.
- *Encourage client summaries.* Keep checking that clients understand how to instruct themselves in the skills you train. Periodically request client summaries of targeted skills.
- *Use handouts, cassettes and videotapes.* Provide clients with learning materials that they can keep, for instance, handouts of specific thinking skills. You can also provide cassettes and videotapes of targeted skills. Where possible, get clients making their own material, for instance, their own coping self-talk cassettes.
- *Encourage clients to keep helping files.* Clients can keep files that record their lifeskills helping journeys, as such files assist memory and revision. Contents of personal helping files can include redefinitions and statements of working goals, plans, clients' session notes, progress reviews, handouts, and homework assignments and answers.
- *Develop clients' skills at identifying and using supports.* Assist clients in recognizing and using existing supports available to them. Where necessary, help clients to develop skills of expanding their support networks. Clients can request that support network members provide honest feedback in constructive ways.

ACTIVITIES

1. Assess the importance of each of the following thinking skills for assessing clients in consolidating trained skills as self-helping skills for after helping:

    imparting a psychological education framework and using skills language;

    owning responsibility for choosing;

    self-instructing;

    using coping self-talk;

    possessing realistic rules;

    perceiving accurately;

    attributing cause accurately;

    predicting realistically;

    goal-setting skills;

    using visualizing;

    using self-reward.

2. Answer the following questions in regard to a client group with whom you either work now or might work in future:

    (a) What is the likelihood of these clients not maintaining their gains after helping ends?

    (b) What are some of the main reasons why these clients might not maintain their gains?

    (c) Before the final helping session, what can you do to increase the chances of clients consolidating trained skills as self-helping skills for after helping?

SEVENTEEN

How to end helping

Great is the art of beginning, but greater the art of ending.
H. W. Longfellow

As highlighted in the previous chapter, lifeskills helping has its endings built into its beginnings. With its emphasis on self-helping, lifeskills helping never ends. However, here to draw some boundaries, I define the ending stage as starting in the second-to-last session and concluding when all scheduled helper–client contact finishes.

FORMATS FOR ENDING HELPING

Choices you have for how to end helping include the following:

- *Predetermined ending.* Helpers and clients may contract for helping to last for a stipulated number of sessions. Sometimes predetermined or fixed endings are by necessity rather than by choice, for instance, when students leave university after their final exams. Predetermined endings can motivate clients to work hard. Possible disadvantages are restriction of focus and insufficient time to be thorough.
- *Open ending with goals attained.* Helping ends when clients and helpers agree that working goals have been attained. In longer-term helping, this may include a thorough grounding in how to approach new problems within the lifeskills helping framework.

- *Faded ending.* The withdrawal of helper assistance is gradual, for instance, from weekly to bi-weekly sessions.
- *Ending with follow-up contact.* Follow-up contact may consist of booster sessions, which are not to teach new skills but to consolidate previously trained ones. You can schedule follow-up phone calls with clients to check on progress and assist with difficulties in implementing skills. In addition, you can be available for follow-up consultations and phone calls initiated by clients. However, beware of encouraging dependency.

KNOWING WHEN TO END

Discussions about when to end helping should start before the final session. Following are four sources of information for helpers and clients to use in assessing when to end. However, if positive changes are recent, it may pay to wait and see if clients maintain them. Inconsistent information, either within or between different sources, merits further exploration. Your decision is easy if all four sources are consistently positive:

- *Client self-report.* Clients say they manage problems better. They report using targeted skills well, and are happier, more confident and less prone to unwanted feelings. They feel ready to manage on their own.
- *Helper observation.* You observe improvements in how clients feel, think and act. They no longer have the symptoms, such as debilitating anxiety, that brought them to helping. They think more realistically about their problems, and seem to act more effectively and to have learned targeted skills well enough to maintain them.
- *Feedback from others.* Other important people in clients' lives give them feedback that they have changed, and people like helpers' aides, spouses, peers or parents make positive reports to you.
- *Attainment of measurable goals.* Sometimes clients' goals are easily measurable, for instance, abstaining from alcohol or losing weight and staying lighter. Some goals may be specific targets, for instance, passing a driving test or going on an aeroplane.

ENDING-STAGE TASKS AND SKILLS

Following are some important ending-stage tasks and skills.

Consolidate trained skills as self-helping skills

The main task of the ending stage is to improve clients' chances of maintaining and developing targeted skills after helping. Even with clients who come for brief helping, you seek to consolidate their learning. Following are some skills of enhancing consolidation in the ending stage.

MAKE TRANSITION STATEMENTS

During helping you may make statements reminding clients of its finiteness. You can introduce the ending stage with one or more transition statements, such as the following:

> Our next session is the final session. Before the session I suggest you review your progress to date and think about any problems you may experience in maintaining your skills in future. Perhaps the main agenda for the final session should be how to help you consolidate your skills for afterwards. Are you happy with this?

SUMMARIZE MAIN LEARNINGS

Clients can summarize both their main learnings and their perceptions of progress. Making personal summaries can be done as homework assignments before final sessions. Clients can write down or cassette-record summaries for future reference. Also, they can cassette-record final sessions.

REHEARSE COPING WITH HIGH-RISK SITUATIONS AND
RETRIEVING LAPSES

Where possible, do not leave rehearsing coping with high-risk situations until the final session. In the ending stage, assist clients in anticipating specific situations in which they still feel vulnerable when using targeted skills. Try to give them a 'high-risk situation' inoculation kit of relevant thinking and action skills. Similarly, help clients to see that they may have lapses, and stress the importance of developing good retrieval skills. Maintaining gains frequently requires overcoming setbacks and obstacles. Consequently, encourage clients to possess a 'hang in there' attitude. Rehearse clients in how to think and act before high-risk situations and after lapses. See that they have relevant information in take-away form, for instance, reminder cards detailing useful skills and coping self-talk.

REINFORCE EFFECTIVE THINKING SKILLS

Use the ending stage to reinforce clients in continuing to work on thinking skills conducive to maintaining and developing targeted skills. Such inner-game skills were outlined in Chapter 16.

EXPLORE ARRANGEMENTS FOR CONTINUING SUPPORT

Ideally, at helping's end clients are able to support themselves. Nevertheless, consider whether clients require some form of continuing support to consolidate skills. Following are possibilities:

- *Further contact with helpers.* Options include follow-up sessions and phone calls at either helpers' or clients' requests.
- *Referral for individual helping.* Despite making considerable progress, some clients may still require further professional assistance. If you are unavailable or think another helper can better assist them, refer such clients.
- *Referral for group helping.* Some clients may gain from joining lifeskills training groups in which they can practise and develop targeted skills. Also, peer self-groups can assist clients in maintaining skills.
- *Use of supports.* If you have used helpers' aides, you can contact them both to review progress and to discuss ways in which they might continue to assist clients. Sometimes three-way meetings between helpers, clients and aides are desirable. Also, you can assist clients in identifying and using other people to support their changes.

- *Use of reading and audiovisual material.* On your own initiative or by request, you can suggest appropriate books, training manuals, audio cassettes and videotapes.

Deal with feelings

Clients may have fears or ambivalent feelings about how they are going to manage without helpers, so facilitate open discussion of clients' fears about the future. Focusing on how to deal with high-risk situations and to retrieve lapses goes some way towards addressing clients' fears. Identify and work with thinking-skills weaknesses that contribute to clients feeling vulnerable about supporting themselves. Clients should feel less vulnerable if, throughout helping, you focused on developing active self-helping skills rather than allowing them to be passive recipients of counsellor-offered help.

Clients may also wish to share feelings about you and the helping process. You may get valuable feedback about how helpful you were. In addition, you can share feelings with clients, for instance, 'I enjoyed working with you.'

End ethically

Many important ethical considerations are present during the ending stage, for instance, the boundaries between personal and professional relationships and the duty to protect vulnerable clients. Most professional associations have ethical codes covering issues in providing helping services. Some Australian, British and American ethical codes are referenced in the bibliography.

Say goodbye

Say goodbye in a business-like, yet friendly way, appropriate to professional rather than to personal relationships. Sloppy goodbyes undo some of your previous good work and make it more difficult to work with clients should future need arise.

ACTIVITIES

1. Work with a partner who role-plays a client with a specific high-risk situation, where, when helping ends, he or she is vulnerable to not using targeted skills. Assist your partner in identifying and developing strategies for coping with the high-risk situation.

    Afterwards, discuss and reverse roles.

2. Work with a partner who role-plays a client in a final session. Assist your client in identifying the first post-helping situation where he or she might fail or have a lapse. Then identify and rehearse the client in appropriate skills, particularly thinking skills, for getting back on track.

    Afterwards, discuss and reverse roles.

3. Work with a partner, agree on what your working goals initially were, and assume that now you are about to begin your fifth and final session. Conduct a final session focused on consolidating his or her self-helping skills by using some of the following skills:

    making a transition statement;

    getting him or her to summarize the main learnings from helping;

    rehearsing coping with high-risk situations and retrieving lapses;

    reinforcing effective thinking skills;

    exploring arrangements for continuing support;

    dealing with feelings;

    saying goodbye.

    Afterwards, discuss and reverse roles.

EIGHTEEN

You can help!

*The meaning of good or bad, or better or worse,
is simply helping or hurting.*
Ralph Waldo Emerson

Welcome to the ending stage of this book. In this chapter I discuss some ways that you can improve your lifeskills helping skills. Like clients, helpers have to work hard to maintain and develop skills.

ASSESS YOUR LIFESKILLS HELPING SKILLS

Throughout helping, skilled helpers evaluate how well they use their helping skills. By your final sessions with clients, you have many sources of information for assessing your skills. Such sources of information include: attendance, client feedback, both intentional and unintentional; perceptions of client progresss; session notes; possibly videotape or audio-cassette feedback; feedback from third parties; and compliance with homework tasks. The more clients you see, the more information you have. When assessing helping skills, beware of inaccurate perceptions – you can be too hard or too easy on yourself. You require a balanced appraisal of your strengths and weaknesses.

Below are some questions relevant to assessing your lifeskills helping skills. When answering, focus on your thinking skills, or inner game, as well as on your action skills, or outer game. The questions refer to Chapters 4 to 17 of this book. Go to the relevant chapters if any of the questions are unclear.

What are my skills strengths and weaknesses in each of the following areas?:
>   offering supportive relationships;
>   identifying and clarifying problems;
>   assessing feelings;
>   assessing thinking skills;
>   assessing action skills;
>   redefining problems in skills terms;
>   stating working goals;
>   planning interventions;
>   delivering interventions;
>   developing thinking skills;
>   developing action skills;
>   focusing on feelings;
>   consolidating self-helping skills;
>   ending helping.

DEVELOP YOUR LIFESKILLS HELPING SKILLS

Once you have assessed your lifeskills helping skills, the next question is how to develop them. Very likely you have targeted specific skills weaknesses and set these as working goals. Remember, you need to develop both your inner and outer games. Following are some suggestions for improving your skills.

Reading

You can enrich your background and keep up to date by reading relevant books and journals. You can read my main text *Practical Counselling and Helping Skills: How to Use the Lifeskills Helping Model* (third edition). Also, examine the selected bibliography at the end of this book. Readers interested in learning more about thinking skills should look at the work of Beck, Ellis, Emery, Lazarus and Meinchenbaum as well as my *Effective Thinking Skills*. Journals provide an excellent means of keeping abreast of helping skills developments, and *Cognitive Therapy and Research* and *Behavior Therapy* are two research journals carrying articles relevant to lifeskills helping. Readers in areas such as psychology, social work, psychiatric nursing, teaching and personnel work should review applied journals in their specialties.

Practising

You can practise on your own, in pairs or in groups. This book's end-of-chapter activities give you a start. I provide a much more thorough set of practical skills exercises and experiments in the *Training Manual for Counselling and Helping Skills*, many of which require a partner. You can join or form a peer support group for developing your lifeskills helping skills. In addition, when seeing clients, you can use and assess your skills.

Training courses and workshops

As more trainers become available, training courses and workshops in lifeskills helping will become more common. Well-led courses in the component skills of lifeskills helping – for instance, supportive relationship skills, assessment skills, and training skills – are worth attending. In addition, courses and workshops on how to work with specific clienteles, such as the unemployed, merit attention.

Supervision

Much of the value of supervised practical experience depends on the quality of supervision. Supervisors specifically trained within the lifeskills helping model should increasingly become available. Also, consider peer supervision either in pairs or in groups.

Personal counselling and lifeskills training

All would-be helpers should consider undergoing disciplined personal counselling from skilled helpers. You can work through some of your own 'stuff' that might interfere with your helping effectiveness. You gain insights into how to help others by learning how to use thinking and action skills in your own life. In addition, observing a skilled helper at first hand should assist you in becoming one yourself. Also, you can enrol in well-led training courses to develop specific lifeskills. A bonus is learning how to train from observing skilled trainers at work.

YOU CAN HELP YOURSELF

Though individual clients may have special skills requirements, most lifeskills that helpers and clients need are the same. You can strengthen yourself and help your clients by developing your own lifeskills. Some of the reasons for working on your lifeskills were mentioned in the section on undergoing personal counselling, namely, dealing with potentially intrusive personal 'stuff' and gaining greater insight into specific lifeskills.

You need work on maintaining and developing your lifeskills. Your happiness and well-being are important; the more effective you are in your daily life, the more energy and attention you are likely to possess for clients. Burned-out and disgruntled helpers do not do their best work. The lifeskills helping model is basically a self-helping model, and truly elegant use of it means being able to apply it to both old and new problems. Helping yourself involves many of the same skills you use for helping clients. The five-stage DASIE model can be modified to CASIE when used for your own or clients self-helping purposes:

C *Confront*, identify and clarify my problem.
A *Assess* my problem and redefine it in skills terms.
S *State* working goals and plan self-helping interventions.
I *Implement* my plan.
E *Evaluate* the consequences of implementing my plan.

Become your own best helper. You can use the CASIE self-helping model to address specific problematic situations – say, an upcoming meeting with difficult colleagues – as well as broader problems, such as managing anger. *Think T!* Figure 18.1 provides a T format self-helping worksheet that you can use as part of this process. When addressing both problems and problematic situations, decide what are your overall goals. Then 'Tee-up' your problem or situation so that you can work on it. You, like all humans, possess psychological skills weaknesses and vulnerabilities. Get to know what they are, for instance, specific unrealistic rules or self-defeating behaviours. This knowledge can assist you in pinpointing how best to think and act to attain your overall goals. Almost certainly, your weaknesses are more likely to be activated when you are tired and under pressure. Aim to prevent problems and problematic situations as well as to manage them.

Problem or situation

_____

_____

Overall goal(s) What ends do I seek to attain?

1. _____ .____

2. _____

3. _____

Redefinition in skills terms What are my actual and potential skills weaknesses?

Thinking-skills weaknesses	Action-skills weaknesses

Statement of working goals What skills can I develop and use to attain my ends?

Thinking-skills goals	Action-skills goals

Figure 18.1   _Lifeskills helping: T-format self-helping worksheet_

POSTSCRIPT

All people possess repertoires of lifeskills strengths and weaknesses. Everyone possesses the potential to help or hurt themselves and others. As helpers you have a special responsibility to develop your helping potential – may the lifeskills helping approach assist you on your personal and helping journals. Some final words of encouragement:

Your contribution is important.

You can make a difference.

You can strengthen both yourself and others.

YOU CAN HELP!

ACTIVITIES

1. For each of DASIE's five stages, assess your strengths and weaknesses in using the lifeskills helping model.
2. State working goals to develop your lifeskills helping skills and plan how to attain them.
3. Pick a specific problematic situation in your life. Apply the lifeskills self-helping CASIE model to it. When doing so, complete a T-format self-helping worksheet.
4. Maintain and develop your DASIE skills for your helping work and your CASIE skills for your personal life. Accept the lifelong challenge to keep and improve both your helping skills and your lifeskills.

Selected Bibliography

Alberti, R.E., and Emmons, M. L. (1990) *Your Perfect Right: A Guide to Assertive Living* (6th edn). San Luis Obispo, CA: Impact Publishers.

Alpert, R., and Haber, R. N. (1960) Anxiety in academic achievement situations. *Journal of Abnormal and Social Psychology*, **61**, 204–15.

American Association for Counselling and Development (1988) *Ethical Standards*. Alexandria, VA: Author.

American Psychiatric Association (1987) *Diagnostic and Statistical Manual of Mental Disorders* (3rd edn – revised). Washington, DC: Author.

American Psychological Association (1987) General guidelines for providers of psychological services. *American Psychologist*, **42**, 724–9.

American Psychological Association (1990) Ethical principles of psychologists. *American Psychologist*, **45**, 390–5.

Argyle, M. (1992) *The Social Psychology of Everyday Life*. London: Routledge.

Argyle, M., and Henderson, M. (1985) *The Anatomy of Relationships*. Harmondsworth: Penguin.

Australian Psychological Society (1986) *Code of Professional Conduct*. Melbourne: Author.

Bandura, A. (1986) *Social Foundations of Thought and Action: A Social Cognitive Theory*. Englewood Cliffs, NJ: Prentice-Hall.

Beck, A. T. (1976) *Cognitive Therapy and the Emotional Disorders*. New York: New American Library.

Beck, A. T. (1988) *Love Is Never Enough: How Couples Can Overcome Misunderstandings, Resolve Conflicts, and Solve Relationship Problems through Cognitive Therapy*. New York: Harper & Row.

Beck, A. T. (1991) Cognitive therapy: a 10-year retrospective. *American Psychologist*, **46**, 368–75.

Beck, A. T., and Emery, G. (1985) *Anxiety Disorders and Phobias: A Cognitive Perspective*, New York: Basic Books.

Beck, A. T., Rush, A. J., Shaw, B. F., and Emery, G. (1979) *Cognitive Therapy of Depression*, New York: John Wiley.

Beck, A. T., and Weishaar, M. E. (1989) Cognitive therapy. In R. J. Corsini and D. Wedding (eds), *Current Psychotherapies* (4th edn. pp. 285–320), Itasca, IL: Peacock.

Bernstein, D. A., and Borkovec, T. D. (1973) *Progressive Relaxation Training: A Manual for the Helping Professions*. Champaign, IL: Research Press.

British Association for Counselling (1990) *Code of Ethics and Practice for Counsellors*. Rugby: Author.

British Psychological Society (1991) *Code of Conduct, Ethical Principles and Guidelines*. Leicester: Author.

Carkhuff, R. R. (1987) *The Art of Helping* (6th edn). Amherst, MA: Human Resource Development Press.

Corey, G., Corey, M. S., and Callanan, P. (1993) *Issues and Ethics in the Helping Professions* (4th edn). Pacific Grove, CA: Brooks/Cole.

Cormier, W. H., and Cormier, L. S. (1991) *Interviewing Strategies for Helpers: Fundamental Skills and Cognitive Behavioural Interventions* (3rd edn) Pacific Grove, CA: Brooks/Cole.

Egan, G. (1990) *The Skilled Helper: A Systematic Approach to Effective Helping* (4th edn). Pacific Grove, CA: Brooks/Cole.

Ellis, A. (1962) *Reason and Emotion in Psychotherapy*. New York: Lyle Stuart.

Ellis, A. (1977) *Anger: How to Live With and Without It*. New York: Lyle Stuart.

Ellis, A. (1989) Rational-emotive therapy. In R. J. Corsini and D. Wedding (eds), *Current Psychotherapies* (4th edn, pp. 197–238), Itasca, IL: Peacock.

Ellis, A., and Harper, R. A. (1975) *A New Guide to Rational Living*. North Hollywood, CA: Wilshire Books.

Emery, G. (1982) *Own Your Own Life*. New York: New American Library.

Frankl, V. E. (1959) *Man's Search for Meaning*. New York: Washington Square Press.

Frankl, V. E. (1969) *The Doctor and the Soul*. Harmondsworth: Penguin.

Frankl, V. E. (1975) *The Unconscious God: Psychotherapy and Theology*. New York: Simon and Schuster.

Gallwey, W. T. (1974) *The Inner Game of Tennis*. London: Pan.

Gendlin, E. T. (1981) *Focusing* (2nd edn). New York: Bantam Books.

Glasser, W. (1965) *Reality Therapy: A New Approach to Psychiatry*. New York: Harper & Row.

Goldfried, M. R., and Davison, G. C. (1976) *Clinical Behavior Therapy*. New York: Holt, Rinehart and Winston.

Holland, J. L. (1973) *Making Vocational Choices: A Theory of Careers*. Englewood Cliffs, NJ: Prentice-Hall.

Hopson, B., and Scally, M. (1981) *Lifeskills Teaching*. London: McGraw-Hill.

Jacobson, E. (1938) *Progressive Relaxation* (2nd edn). Chicago: University of Chicago Press.

Jacobson, E. (1976) *You Must Relax*. Boston: Unwin Paperbacks.

Kanfer, F. H., and Goldstein (eds) (1991) *Helping People Change: A Textbook of Methods* (4th edn). Oxford: Pergamon Press.

Kazdin, A. E. (1989) *Behavior Modification in Applied Settings* (4th edn). Pacific Grove, CA: Brooks/Cole.

King, M. L. (1963) *Strength to Love*. Philadelphia, PA: Fortress Press.

Lazarus, A. A. (1977) *In the Mind's Eye*. New York: The Guilford Press.

Lewinsohn, P. M., Munoz, R. F., Youngren, M. A., and Zeiss, A. M. (1986) *Control Your Depression* (rev. edn). New York: Prentice Hall Press.

Maslow, A. H. (1962) *Towards a Psychology of Being*. New York: Van Nostrand.

Maslow, A. H. (1970) *Motivation and Personality*. (2nd edn). New York: Harper & Row.

May, R., and Yalom, I. D. (1989) Existential psychotherapy. In R. J. Corsini and D. Wedding (eds), *Current Psychotherapies* (4th edn, pp. 363–402), Itasca, IL: Peacock.

Meichenbaum, D. H. (1977) *Cognitive-Behavior Modification: An Integrative Approach*. New York: Plenum.

Meichenbaum, D. H. (1983) *Coping with Stress*. London: Century Publishing.

Meichenbaum, D. H. (1985) *Stress Inoculation Training*. New York: Pergamon Press.

Meichenbaum, D. H., and Deffenbacher, J. L. (1988) Stress inoculation training. *The Counseling Psychologist*, **16**, 69–90.

MIMS (latest edition). Middlesex: Haymarket Publishing, and Australian MIMS, 68 Alexandra Street, Crows Nest, Sydney, Australia.

National Board for Certified Counselors (1987) *Code of Ethics*. Alexandria, VA: Author.

Nelson-Jones, R. (1989) *Effective Thinking Skills: Preventing and Managing Personal Problems*. London: Cassell.

Nelson-Jones, R. (1991) *Lifeskills: A Handbook*. London: Cassell.

Nelson-Jones, R. (1993) *Practical Counselling and Helping Skills: How to Use the Lifeskills Helping Model* (3rd edn). London: Cassell.

Nelson-Jones, R. (1993) *Relating Skills: Revised Second Edition of Human Relationship Skills*. London: Cassell.

Nelson-Jones, R. (1993) *Training Manual for Counselling and Helping Skills*. London: Cassell.

Pfeiffer, J. W., Jones, J., and Goodstein, L. (1972–92) *Developing Human Resources* (annual sets). San Diego, CA.: University Associates.

Raskin, N. J., and Rogers, C. R. (1989) Person-centred therapy. In R. J. Corsini and D. Wedding (eds), *Current Psychotherapies* (4th edn, pp. 155–94), Itasca, IL: Peacock.

Rogers, C. R. (1951) *Client-Centered Therapy*. Boston: Houghton Mifflin.

Rogers, C. R. (1957) The necessary and sufficient conditions of therapeutic personality change. *Journal of Consulting Psychology*, 21, 95–103.

Rogers, C. R. (1961) *On Becoming a Person*. Boston: Houghton Mifflin.

Rogers, C. R. (1980) *A Way of Being*. Boston: Houghton Mifflin.

Seligman, M. E. P. (1990) *Learned Optimism*. London: Random House.

Tillich, P. (1952) *The Courage to Be*. New Haven: Yale University Press.

Wolpe, J. E. (1982) *The Practice of Behavior Therapy* (3rd edn). New York: Pergamon Press.

Yalom, I. D. (1980) *Existential Psychotherapy*. New York: Basic Books.

Index

acceptance
    attitude of respect and   35–6
    avoiding unrewarding 'don'ts'   44
    sending good body messages   36–7
anxiety
    assessment of   62–3
    managing feelings of   171–5
    managing speech anxiety   118
assessment
    of action skills   82–8
    of feelings   60–8
    of helping skills   191–2
    reasons for   60–1, 69
    redefining problems   10–14
    self-monitoring   76, 86, 149–51, 182
    supportive relationships in   11, 64–5
    of thinking skills   69–81
    use of role playing in   66, 77–8, 85
assigning homework, skills for   17–18,
    93, 126–7, 183

Beck, A.T.   9, 192
Beecher, Henry Ward   60
Berlin, Irving   178

Bernstein, D.   15
body messages
    attending behaviour   37
    sending   36–7, 48–57, 83, 170
    as speaking skill   119–20
    understanding feelings from   41–3
Borkovic, T.D.   15

Carkhuff, R.R.   6
CASIE self-helping model   194–6
challenging, see confronting
Cleaver, Eldridge   46
coaching skills   17–18, 123–5
confidentiality   28–9
confronting
    inauthenticity   165–6
    skills of   53–7
    managing initial resistances   58–9
consolidating self-helping skills
    assigning homework   17–18, 126–7,
      183
    during helping   17–18, 20, 181–3
    in ending stage   20
    planning for   182–3

continuation messages, as small rewards
39–40
contracts, negotiating plans 113
coping self-talk 8, 25, 70, 120–1,
132–4, 167, 169, 172, 180
culture
cultural empathy 30–1, 58
cultural skills 30–1
helper's culture 30–1

Darwin, Charles 69
DASIE model of helping
brief helping 21
extended helping 21
flexibility in using 20–1
stages in 7–21
decision-making
developing skills of 144–5
planning interventions 109–14
demonstration
methods of 120–2
skills of 122–3

Egan, G. 6
Ellis, A. 9, 75, 192
Emerson, Ralph Waldo 22, 191
Emery, G. 192
ending stage
agendas for 187–9
deciding when to end 186
formats for 19, 185–6
skills for enhancing consolidation
20, 187–9
Erasmus 89
ethics 28–9, 189
exercises and games 158–9
expressing feelings
interventions for 168–70
showing involvement 58

feedback, dimensions of 124–5
Fuller, Thomas 1

genuineness
self-disclosure 58
sending consistent messages 37
goals
characteristics 98
see also stating working goals
Goethe, J.W. 147
graded task assignment 124, 151–2

Holland, J.L. 23
homework, assigning skills 17–18,
126–7, 183
Huxley, T.H. 82

internal viewpoint 34–5, 40
interventions for developing action skills
develop self-monitoring skills
149–51
exercises and games 158–9
identify and use supports 160
personal experiments 154–6
rehearsal, methods of 152–3
role-playing 124, 153–4
sequence graded tasks 124, 151–2
timetable activities 156–8
use helper's aides 159–60
interventions for developing thinking
skills
attributing cause accurately 138–40
choosing realistic personal rules
134–6
coping self-talk 132–4
making decisions rationally 144–5
owning responsibility for choosing
131–2
perceiving accurately 136–8

predicting realistically 140–1
setting realistic goals 141–2
visualizing skills 142–3
interventions focusing on feelings
experiencing feelings 163–8
expressing feelings 168–70
managing anxiety 171–5
managing feelings 170–5
medication 176
relaxation skills 173–5
systematic desensitization 175

Kaiser, Henry J. 6

language
of feelings 41–3
skills language 4, 8–9, 21, 90,
99–100
Lao-Tse 162
Lazarus, A.A., 192
lifeskills
defining 3–4
maintaining 6
lifeskills helping
assumptions 1, 6
goals 1
language 1
people-centredness 1
psychological education
framework 1
lifeskills helpers
culture and cultural awareness 30–1
ethics 28–9, 189
feelings 26–7
as feelings educators 162–3
helping experiences 24
inner and outer games 8, 21, 24–6,
30
motives 22
race 31

sex-role identity and expectations
27–8
sexuality and sexual orientation 27
social class 31
thinking skills 24–6, 44, 99–101
values of 28–9
listening
importance of 34, 64–5
rewarding listening skills 34–45,
165
teaching inner listening 166–7
see also reflective responding
Longfellow, H.W. 185

Marcus Aurelius 129
medication 176
Meichenbaum, D.H. 9, 192
messages, kinds of 82–3

openers 38–9

permission to talk 47–8
personal responsibility 3, 19, 70, 163
planning interventions
categories of plans 15–16, 111—12
choosing interventions 109–11,
182–3
helper skills for 112–14, 182–3
problematic skills
changing 6
DASIE (a five-stage model) 6–21
defining 6, 11–13
and problem management 6, 98
psychological education framework 1
psychophysiological disorders 63
PTC framework 75, 84–5, 138
Publilius Syrus 108

questioning skills
  areas for questions   50–1
  types of questions   11, 40, 51–3,
    65–6, 76–7, 165

redefining problems in skills terms
  examples of   13
  skills for   11–13, 89–96, 182
referral   111, 188
reflective responding
  defining   40
  reflecting feelings   41–3
  reflecting feelings and reasons   43–4
  rewording   40–1
  teaching inner listening   166–7
rehearsal
  methods of   152–3
  role-playing   152–4
  visualized   153
relationship skills
  offering a supportive relationship   8,
    11, 17–18, 64–5, 118, 129–30, 148,
    181
  and training skills   16–17, 118
relaxation
  brief self-instructions   174–5
  mental relaxation   143, 175
  progressive muscular   174
  systematic desensitization   175
repetition phenomenon   6, 98, 129
resistances
  managing initial   58–9
  to working on action skills   148–9
rewarding listening
  functions of   34, 64–5, 165
  skills of   34–45
Rogers, C.R.   23, 25
role-playing
  in assessment   66, 77–8, 85
  in developing action skills   153–4

self-disclosing   58
self-helping
  consolidating skills   178–83, 187–9
  as goal of counselling and helping   6
sex role
  androgyny   28
  expectations   28–9
  gender-awareness   28
  identity   27–9
sexuality
  of helper   27
  sexual orientation   27
Shaw, George Bernard   116, 162
speaking skills
  delivery skills   119–20
  managing speech anxiety   118
  preparing clear content   119
specificity
  clarifying problems   46–7, 49–50, 182
  identifying problems   46–7, 50–3
  redefining problems in skills terms
    11–13, 91, 182
stages in helping, DASIE model   7–21
stating working goals
  considerations in   14–15, 98–9, 182
  helper action skills for   101–3
  helper thinking skills for   99–101
  problem management goals   98
  problematic skills goals   98
  risks of   98–9
STC framework   75, 77, 84–5, 135, 138
structuring skills   8–9, 47–8, 181
summarizing skills   53–5, 183
supervision   193
support
  developing client's support networks
    160, 188–9
  for helpers   159–60, 188, 193
  in helping relationships   8, 11,
    17–18, 33–45, 64–5, 118, 129–30,
    148, 181
systematic desensitization   175

thinking skills
  assessment of   69–81
  attributing cause accurately   8, 25–6,
    72, 80, 100, 138–40, 167, 169, 180
  coping self-talk   8, 25, 70, 120–1,
    132–4, 167, 169, 172, 180
  decision-making skills   8, 144–5
  inner and outer games   8, 21, 24–6,
    30
  for managing anxiety   171–3
  owning responsibility for choosing
    8, 70, 80, 131–2, 167, 169, 180
  perceiving accurately   8, 25, 71–2,
    80, 101, 136–8, 167, 169, 172, 180
  possessing realistic personal rules   8,
    25, 71, 80, 100–1, 134–6, 167, 169,
    172, 180
  predicting realistically   8, 72, 80,
    101, 140–1, 167, 169, 172, 180
  in rewarding listening   44–5
  setting realistic goals   8, 73–4,
    141–2, 167, 169, 172, 180
  in stating working goals   99–101
  visualizing skills   73, 142–3, 167,
    169, 172, 180
timetabling   156–7

timing
  of interventions   109, 113
  managing initial resistances   58–9
training skills
  assigning homework skills   17–18,
    126–7, 183
  coaching skills   17–18, 123–5
  demonstration skills   17–18, 120–3
  offering supportive relationships
    17–18, 118
  speaking skills   17–18, 118–20

understanding context skills   58

verbal messages
  avoiding unrewarding 'don'ts'   44
  preparing clear content   119
voice messages
  in rewarding listening   37–8, 48
  as speaking skill   119–20

whiteboard, use of   9–10, 78, 91–2, 102

Zeno of Citium   32